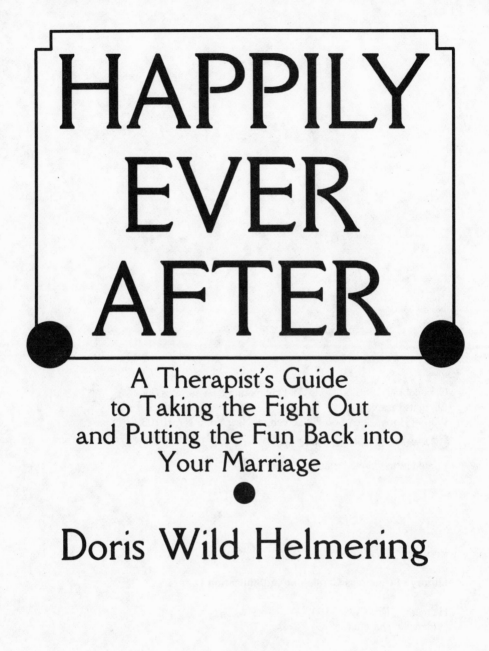

HAPPILY EVER AFTER

A Therapist's Guide
to Taking the Fight Out
and Putting the Fun Back into
Your Marriage

Doris Wild Helmering

WARNER BOOKS

A Warner Communications Company

Copyright © 1986 by Doris Wild Helmering & Associates, Inc.
All rights reserved.
Warner Books, Inc., 666 Fifth Avenue, New York, NY 10103

W A Warner Communications Company

Printed in the United States of America

Book design: H. Roberts

Library of Congress Cataloging in Publication Data

Helmering, Doris Wild, 1942–
  Happily ever after.

  Bibliography: p. 232
  Includes index.
  1. Marriage—United States. 2. Communication in
marriage. 3. Interpersonal relations. 4. Marriage
counseling—United States. I. Title.
HQ734.H475 1986   646.7′8   85-40911
ISBN 0-446-51351-2

To Skeeter
A Special Person

. . . with love

ACKNOWLEDGMENTS

When I first started writing this book, I had no idea of the work that lay ahead. Had it not been for my family and numerous friends, I couldn't have done it.

I want to especially thank my husband, Skeeter, who read every revision and gave me excellent suggestions on how I might rearrange things or make them more clear. And I didn't always take his suggestions as graciously as I might have. Never once did he get angry and say, "The heck with you." He sat until I dried my tears and got my courage back so I could write some more. He also watched our daughter and took her to the park, cooked our Sunday dinners, brought me coffee, and sent me flowers five different times during the course of my writing this book. Talk about support! Skeeter, thank you. You are truly special.

I also want to thank Kathy Meder, who typed, and typed, and typed. Kathy, you not only do terrific work (and on schedule), but you gave me feedback on the manuscript, support when I needed it, and most important, you gave of yourself in a hundred different ways. What a friend you've become.

To Germaine Eley, I wonder how you could stand me after a while. I needed to talk again and again about my theory on script positions and competitive behaviors. And all those times when I said, "Got a minute?" you proceeded to give me an hour. Without your astute questioning, I would still be trying to sort it all out. Also, thanks for letting me stay at your place when I needed to get away and really knock out some work. I'm always telling people what a smart woman you are and what a terrific friend. Now I have a chance to put it in print.

Paul Helmering, you certainly did a lot of grocery shopping and baby-sitting during the time I worked on this book. And I still remember when you sat and read the manuscript for clarity and said enthusiastically, "This is neat, Mom." Thanks, Son.

Thanks to John Meder for your continual support during the writing of this book. And thanks for all the time you shuttled the manuscript between my house and yours and back again. I wonder how many miles you put on your car?

More thank-yous to Serra Bording-Jones, my partner in practice, who gave me a lot of moral support and kept telling me, "It will be fine." Thanks, too, Serra, for handling the office when I was out writing, having vases of flowers when I returned, and proofing the entire manuscript five times around. You're a wonderful friend and a neat woman.

April Oppliger, my optimistic sister, who kept saying, "Keep writing—your book will help everyone." Thanks.

Thanks, Mom and Dad, for all the baby-sitting you did while I wrote this book. Thanks also, Neen, for all the loving care you gave to Anna Mary. You're not only good parents but very good grandparents.

They say literary agents don't give courses in writing, but you did, Elise Simon Goodman. Your first comment, "Not enough connective tissue," was exactly the direction I needed in order to do the first rewrite of the book. And your next comment, "Not focused enough," pushed me to do a second rewrite. Thanks, Elise, for believing in me and in this project.

David Gosnell, I didn't even know you when I started writing this book. And when I needed an opinion about the material from someone who didn't know me, you read the manuscript. I still remember your telephone call a week later when you said enthusiastically, "I love it!" How I used those words to shore me up during my third rewrite.

Claire Zion, my editor at Warner, you are so smart. Your questions about the manuscript were invaluable, for they nudged me to give the book the final focus it needed. Also, your enthusiasm is contagious. I love working with women like you.

I also want to thank Roger McWilliams, who was my St. Louis editor. Your suggestions, easygoing manner, and fast turnaround time were a good combination for me.

Ed Sedarbaum, you're a superb copy editor.

Les Grodsky, thanks for all those pats on the back, accompanied by, "You can do it, kid." Thanks, too, for taking some of the therapy groups when I was out writing. You've always been a support to me.

Thanks to therapists Michaeleen Cradock and Ann Weisman, who led some of the other therapy groups when I was away writing.

Nancy Ackley, thanks. Your belief in me was a real support.

Thanks John Helmering, Judy Cassidy, Susan Fryer, Martha Scharff, and Mary Jane Lamping for your support and for proofing the galleys. What a fine job each of you did! Each of you is very special.

Anna Mary, thanks for all those sweet drawings you made for me and all those love notes you brought to me as I sat writing. I'm so happy to have a daughter such as you.

I also thank all the people who have given of themselves through their stories, as well as all the people who filled out the script questionnaires and took the Script Position Tests. It is your stories that have made this book truly human. And it is your stories that will allow others to grow and change and make their marriages better.

Each of you has played a special part in making my dream, *Happily Ever After*, come true.

TABLE OF CONTENTS

AUTHOR'S NOTE

The material in this book is based primarily on communication theory, Transactional Analysis, and my own theory, which I have developed and refined over the years. The case histories that appear are those of people I have seen for marriage counseling, group therapy, or individual therapy. All names are changed. Occasionally some details have been altered to protect individuals' identities and those of their families. In a few instances the cases are a composite of two individuals. Any similarity between these case histories and the problems of another couple or individual is purely coincidental, but understandable, since we all struggle in some fashion or another with many of these same issues.

When a behavior traditionally has been associated with men, I have used the pronoun *he*. When a behavior traditionally has been associated with women, I have used *she*. These pronouns are also used alternately. By no means do I intend to imply at any point that certain behaviors are exclusively true of one sex or the other. Both sexes are equally capable of all the behaviors I discuss in this book, and my use of pronouns should be viewed only as a literary convenience.

Some terms appear in this book that will not be familiar to you; therefore, I have included a Glossary in the back of the book for your reference. Each word that is listed in the Glossary is marked with an asterisk the first time it appears in the text. The words *marriage counseling*, *therapy*, and *counseling* are used interchangeably.

INTRODUCTION

This book was written for anyone who wants to improve his or her marriage, or a relationship with another person. By reading this book and answering the questions and quizzes throughout, you will come to understand things about yourself, your mate, and the interactions that occur between the two of you that make your marriage what it is today. But more importantly, you will come to understand how you can make your marriage a better one for tomorrow.

The information presented here is identical to the information people get when they see me for marriage counseling. The only difference is in the way it is presented. In my office during a one-hour session, I can use information from any chapter as the need arises. And frequently I'll use bits and pieces of information from seven or eight chapters in one session in order to help a couple understand what's really going on in their relationship. In the book, I'll introduce you to one subject at a time and then devote an entire chapter to explaining the material. Seeing me face to face in counseling versus reading this book is similar to going to a particular country to learn their language versus learning that language in a classroom. If you go to a country to learn a language, everything gets thrown at you at one time. In the classroom, you're introduced to nouns and then verbs and then sentence structure. Either way the end result is the same: You learn the language. The process is different; the result is the same.

You will learn about your Secret Game Plan* (all marriages have them) and how destructive it can be to your relationship. You'll not only learn to spot questions with hidden agendas,* but you'll find out how to respond to such a question when it comes your way. You'll learn to identify psychological games such as I'll-Do-It-When-I-Get-Damn-Good-And-Ready, Sweetheart and Now-I've-Got-You, You-S.O.B., and you'll find out *why* you and your mate play these games and what payoffs you get from playing them. You'll learn how early childhood experiences influenced your choice of a partner, as well as how the early years of your life impact your marriage today. You'll find out what script position* you take in your relationship: Caretaker,* Passive Taker,* Corrector,* or Passive Aggressive.* You'll discover how you and your spouse compete for attention and control, and you'll learn how to better handle this competition when it comes up. You'll be able to spot when you're on the Drama Triangle,* and you'll see how you are a Rescuer,* a Victim,* and a Persecutor* in your marriage. You'll come to understand how feelings are sometimes inappropriately used in a relationship. You'll take your stroke count, and you'll learn how many positive strokes* and negative strokes* are exchanged in your relationship. You'll come to think in terms of options. You'll learn to analyze and look beyond a particular problem. And perhaps most important, you'll come to see how *if you change, your spouse's response to you will change, and your marriage will get better.*

IF YOU CHANGE,
YOUR RELATIONSHIP CHANGES

People often feel stuck when things aren't going particularly well in their relationship because they think they can't possibly make it better. Their spouse is not willing to go to a marriage counselor, read a book, or even sit down and discuss the problems in the marriage. So how can things get better? Things get better because you change, and as a result of your changing, your marriage will change and get better.

For example, one woman I saw in therapy said that no matter what issue she confronted her husband on, they wound up having a

*Each word that is listed in the Glossary is marked with an asterisk the first time it appears in the text.

major fight. She would comment on something he did or didn't do, such as not cleaning off his papers from the dining table as he had promised. He would respond to her confrontation by presenting her with a list of things she hadn't done. And they would be off and running, with him attacking and her defending. Unfortunately, the original issue of cleaning off his papers from the dining table was never solved. This woman learned that when she raised an issue and her husband went on the attack about something she hadn't done, she should remain calm and say, "That's not the issue." Or she should say, "I'm willing to discuss that, but first let's deal with the issue of cleaning your papers off the dining room table."

By sticking to the issue and refusing to discuss any other subject until the original one was resolved, this woman was able to keep the discussion from escalating into a major fight. As she changed, the marriage got better.

Another man used to be supercritical of his wife. No matter what she did, he would find fault with it. She got back at him by refusing to visit his parents. This annoyed him no end. And when he went to family gatherings alone, he felt "downright foolish." Once this man knocked off his critical remarks and started saying more positive things to his wife, she started visiting the in-laws again. He changed, and their relationship changed.

Certainly if one's partner is in love with someone else and refuses to give up that relationship, or one's mate is an alcoholic or is involved in some other chemical abuse and refuses to give up the addiction, or one's spouse is physically abusive, it will be difficult to turn things around. If you are in one of these situations, you will need more help than this book has to offer and you should see someone professionally. You are too important to let a destructive situation continue. You may find, too, that in reading this book you will get the courage to seek the professional help you need.

SOME PAIN, BUT A GREAT DEAL OF GAIN

As you read this book, I'll be asking you to answer certain questions about yourself and your relationship. I think it best that you write down your answers, since this will help you focus more on yourself and your marriage. If writing down the answers is distracting or you feel the information is too personal to be shared by someone else who may read the book, then answer the questions in your head. The important thing is that you answer the questions if you want to get everything out of the book that it has to offer.

It's best to read the book from front to back the first time around because the information is "progressive" in that each chapter presupposes an understanding of the earlier chapters. Also, the earlier chapters don't evoke as many feelings as the later ones. Understandably you will find some chapters more on target and helpful to your marriage, and those chapters you'll probably want to reread and refer to from time to time.

As you go through the book, you'll find that I always make specific suggestions as to how you might behave differently in order to solve a particular problem. Some suggestions I'll make for changing your behavior will be relatively easy for you to follow. Others will be more difficult because you've been relating to your partner in a certain way for a long time, and to behave differently is going to take a conscious, concerted effort on your part. But if you read the book and follow the suggestions you'll change, and your marriage will improve.

One thing you will find in reading this book is that although there will be parts of the book you'll "love," there will be other parts that you may not love or even like. It's difficult sometimes to take a look at your behavior and say, "I do that. No wonder there's a problem." For me it was easy to admit that I was a Caretaker even though that's not good for one's marriage (you'll see why later). But it was difficult for me to admit that I was too critical, and that I played Corrector far too often in my marriage. I think a friend summed it up best when she said, "I'm not sure I want to know everything I'm learning from reading this book. I'm beginning to see too many things I do that cause problems." What's good, however, is that once you see what's going on, you can behave differently.

Because some people have experienced uncomfortable feelings while reading this book, I ask that you take care of yourself. If you begin to feel sad, anxious, or angry while reading certain sections, give yourself permission to talk with someone. Talking helps dissipate uncomfortable feelings, and in the course of talking you may actually resolve the issue.

I do think you'll find a greater tolerance for yourself and your spouse as you read, since you'll come to understand *why* you both behave as you do. At the same time, you'll probably find yourself becoming less tolerant because once you know what's going on in your relationship, you'll expect everything to change. Unfortunately, no matter how much you want it, change just doesn't happen overnight. People need time to change and turn their behavior around. So you'll have some days of aggravation and disappointment, both with yourself and your spouse. You may even find that things will get worse in your relationship for a time because all this new information will tend to make you picky about what your spouse is doing. Moreover, you'll have a label for his or her behavior. Also, as you struggle to change your behavior, your spouse may be subconsciously struggling to keep the status quo. But if you keep focusing on yourself, and telling yourself it is *you* that must change, you'll get through this difficult time. And it will be well worth it.

In marriage counseling, I constantly stress that everything is a trade-off. In using this book, you will trade in the pain of a not particularly satisfying marriage for the pain of changing your behavior. In the long run, however, I think you'll find this to be worthwhile. If you go through the pain of changing your behavior, your marriage will improve and the pain will disappear. If, on the other hand, you decide to reject the pain that accompanies change, you still have the pain of being in an unsatisfying marriage, day in, day out.

I hope you'll have the courage to use this book and change yourself in order that your marriage changes. Few things equal the special joy that comes with having a good marriage.

1

WELCOME TO MARRIAGE COUNSELING

Generally, one of the first things I do when someone comes for marriage counseling is to introduce myself and then ask, "How come you're here?" Often the person says, "It's my marriage. It's not working. I'm not happy, and I don't know what to do about it anymore. I know I don't want to get out of my marriage, but things can't go on the way they are."

After getting basic information on how long the person has been married, if he has any children, and if he has had therapy before, I ask what problems he sees in his marriage. At this point the person usually focuses on his spouse and gives me a list of things that the spouse does or doesn't do that cause problems in the marriage. If both the husband and wife come in for counseling, I ask each of them what they see as the problem. Almost invariably, each will see the other as the problem.

In addition, I immediately start focusing on the interaction between the two of them. As I work with an individual or a couple, I'm constantly bombarding them with feedback about their behavior, and continually asking them to analyze why they behave as they do, what they get from behaving this way, and what they can do differently to make their marriage better.

I also assign homework at the end of each counseling session; during the week I want people to think about their therapy and focus on themselves and their behavior. Also, I expect a person to start

7

making some immediate behavioral changes. And in a week they will start to feel and see a difference in their marriage.

FIRST SESSIONS

Here are some examples of what takes place in a first session in marriage counseling. These examples will give you an idea of how the counseling process works and the issues you'll be addressing as you read through the book. I purposely chose three individuals, as opposed to couples who are working on their marriage, to show you that *one person can change the relationship.*

Kate

When Kate comes for her first session in marriage counseling without her husband (he is unwilling to come), she complains that he never approaches her sexually. When I say, "Never?" she laughs and replies, "Well, almost never."

Apparently, three or four months would pass before her husband would approach her. Kate would like to have sex more frequently— about once a week. If she approaches him, they might have sex, but this also causes her problems, because even when they have sex, he really doesn't take care of her. Once he achieves orgasm, he immediately becomes disinterested in her and whether or not she has orgasm. He seems concerned only with his sexual needs.

Kate also complains that her husband doesn't initiate anything physical. He doesn't put his arm around her, hold her hand, or hug her. Another problem is that he rarely gives her compliments.

Kate, on the other hand, believes she meets all his needs and wants. She does whatever he asks; she compliments him; she hugs him; she approaches him sexually; she buys him little presents; she cooks and makes his favorite dessert; she keeps the house clean; she works outside the home and contributes to the family finances; she makes all the social plans; she arranges for the baby-sitter. And she also keeps herself looking nice.

When I ask her how she has tried to solve these problems in the past, Kate says she has had countless discussions with her husband, at least a few thousand. But these discussions never seemed to go anywhere; he would promise to change but didn't. She also confesses to having had countless temper tantrums over these issues that later left her persecuting herself for her bad behavior. Then, because she had said so many ugly things to him during her tantrums, she would try to be extra nice to make up for the way she had acted. His behavior, however, never seemed to change.

Over the years they had made pacts with each other. Kate would agree to do things to please her husband, and he would agree to approach her sexually once a week and compliment her. Typically, she would keep her bargain, but he wouldn't keep his. At this point she feels at her wit's end.

When I ask her what she likes about her husband, Kate says he almost never criticizes her, never gets angry, and never loses his temper, whereas she is much more "all over the place." He also is a good father and a good provider and he helps around the house if she asks. He is loyal and trustworthy, and she doesn't worry about him running around on her. He also has a good sense of humor, although he doesn't talk with her nearly as much as she would like.

I ask if she has done anything in the past that she considered effective in getting her husband to change. Without hesitation she says, "Yes, when I get quiet. It doesn't take more than half a day and he's giving me attention. He asks how I feel, he hugs me, and generally he seems to be tuned in to me emotionally. Sometimes he even approaches me sexually. As long as I stay somewhat distant from him, he gives me attention. But when I start being nice to him again, it's the same old story."

I tell Kate I suspect several things are going on in their relationship. Her husband seems to be afraid of being close and actively avoids those behaviors that potentially could bring them emotionally closer. It also appears that both are in a power struggle; the more she wants something, the less willing he is to give it to her.

I also suspect that Kate is *too* efficient and that on a subconscious* level her husband may resent her efficiency. Although it might seem ludicrous, his refusal to approach her sexually and to give her compliments and hugs might be the only way he feels in control or has any power in the marriage.

Obviously both of them have an anger problem, since both deal with this feeling inappropriately. Her husband doesn't keep his agreements, which is Passive Aggressive. His behavior is angry, but he is expressing it passively by simply not doing what he agreed to do. I suspect that in his childhood he must have decided that the outright expression of anger is not acceptable, so he learned to deal with this feeling more subtly.

On the other hand, Kate, by her own admission, gets *too* angry. I ask her what her husband does when she confronts him about not keeping the agreements he has made with her. She says he simply sits there looking a bit "hangdog," which makes her even more outraged. I realize then that this couple has a covert agreement that Kate will get angry for both of them.

I ask Kate about her childhood, how anger had been handled in her family, and what kind of a relationship her parents had. She says her parents had a poor relationship, and although they stayed together, they fought almost constantly and someone was always angry. Everyone in her family except an older brother had a bad temper. These angry displays that Kate witnessed in childhood seem to account for the fact that every time Kate feels any negative emotion, she turns the feeling into anger.

Although I understand her anger with her husband when he doesn't keep his agreements, I also expect her to feel sad and disappointed, feelings she says she rarely experiences. I then go back to the fact that her husband has shown more interest when she has withdrawn from him. I know he is feeling her withdrawal in some way. Perhaps if she would take less care of him, he might come around and take more care of her.

Kate agrees with my evaluation but says that the hardest thing for her is to do *less* in the relationship. I say I understand, but it also seems that the hardest thing for her husband is to do *more* in the relationship. If indeed she wants him to take better care of her, she needs to do less.

I then suggest that she do several things differently in the coming week. She could give her husband a hug or a compliment, but then she must wait until he gives her a hug or a compliment. I am pretty sure he will come around, but it will take him a while, and probably longer than she will want to wait or has been willing to wait previously. But no matter how great her desire to jump in and give him a hug or a compliment, she must wait until it is her turn.

I explain to Kate that she and her husband, like all people, need a certain amount of recognition each day, and at present it looks as though she does most of the recognizing—positively, negatively, verbally, and physically. If Kate would do less in the relationship, if she would give her husband less recognition, her husband would soon feel the absence of her input, and he would subconsciously focus on her to get more recognition for himself. He might also approach her sexually, as he had in the past, when she backed away from him.

I suspect that when Kate's husband does take care of her, she responds by being too grateful. The result is that he starts to feel smothered and backs away. So unknowingly, Kate actually sabotages getting taken care of by her husband. I think Kate also has a problem with being emotionally close to her husband because her parents fought constantly and did not provide her with a good model for closeness.

I ask Kate to agree not to allow herself to lose her temper in the coming week. I explain that this is because when she loses her temper, she is acting out and expressing some of her husband's anger. In addition, she gives her husband a lot of attention when she has a temper tantrum—not positive attention but attention nonetheless—which inadvertently serves to cut down on the amount of attention he gives her. She also reinforces her own anger, since anger builds anger.

With the session nearly over, I review the three things that Kate has agreed to do differently in the coming week to change her marriage. She will (1) give a hug or compliment only after she gets one, (2) approach her husband sexually only if he has approached her the previous time, and (3) not have any temper tantrums.

Before leaving, Kate says jokingly, "I hope you realize that you're dooming me to no sex for the week. But come hell or high water, I'm going to keep to my list and see what develops." Once again I make a pitch for Kate to stick to her list. I tell her that sex is a form of recognition, and by her own admission her husband has approached her sexually when she has given him less recognition. So as far as no sex for the week, we'll see what develops.

I make another appointment with Kate, knowing what a hard job she has ahead of her.

In the coming weeks we will explore her early childhood, how she became a Caretaker in her marriage, how she tries to manipulate her husband with her anger, how she feels like a Victim and then turns Persecutor, and how her efficiency actually creates a distance in her marriage. Keeping her list is only the beginning.

Richard

When I ask Richard why he has come to marriage counseling, he laughs and says, "Because my wife sent me." Then he says that his marriage is the pits, and all he and his wife seem to do is argue. When I ask what they argue about, he says they can argue about anything, including how she keeps the house, how they handle their money, how he handles the children, how she doesn't take care of herself (she's overweight), and how he doesn't make enough money.

I ask Richard why his wife didn't come to the session with him. He replies, "She thinks I need to clean up my act first, and then she'll come in and clean up hers."

When I ask what he thinks about this, he says that of the two of them, he is probably the worse. So immediately I ask what he needs to do differently. "I need to be less of a slob," he says. "I need to knock off the sarcastic comments, and I guess I need to help more around the house." When I ask what being less of a slob means, he says picking up his underwear and throwing it down the clothes chute, not leaving his shoes in the middle of the floor where his wife can fall over them, cleaning up his mess after he makes a snack, and rinsing his whiskers down the washbasin after he shaves in the morning. As to what he should do around the house, he says his wife likes it when he gives the girls a bath and tucks them in at night. She's also happy when he helps with the dishes instead of flopping in front of the television right after dinner.

Richard knows exactly what he needs to do differently in his marriage to make it better. Before his session is over, we have made the agreement that in the following week Richard will keep his clothes picked up, his shoes put away, and his whiskers out of the washbasin. He also will help his wife with the dishes and bathe the girls three times a week without being asked. And sarcasm is out; any sarcastic comments he makes he will write down and bring to our next session. Writing them down will make him more conscious of what he's doing and will help him take responsibility for his sarcasm.

If Richard keeps his list, his marriage will undoubtedly start to improve.

James

When I see James for marriage counseling and ask what he needs to do differently in his marriage to make it better, he tells me he's not sure. But when I ask him what his wife complains about, he is able to rattle off a list of things she doesn't like: "She thinks that I don't love her and that I'm too critical of her. But I do love her, and I only get critical when she says something dumb. And it drives her crazy that I run around after her, turning off the lights. But with the cost of electricity, who wouldn't turn off the lights?"

So James knows what his wife wants. But as soon as he tells me what she wants, he dismisses it with a rationale for his own behavior.

I clearly have a Corrector (a person who is highly critical) on my hands. I ask James who criticized him when he was a child; he says his father was terribly critical. "But what does that have to do with the price of mustard?" he jokes. (Now he's criticizing the way I do therapy.) I explain that if someone is criticized as a child, he usually is critical as an adult. He criticizes his spouse, and his spouse criticizes him back, which is a perfect way for him to reexperience those old familiar feelings of childhood when he was criticized. It all fits together like a puzzle.

When I ask James what he does to show his wife that he loves her, he responds: "I make a good salary, I come home on time, I don't play around, and I don't go out and get drunk." But what he doesn't do is compliment her, bring her little surprises, tell her he loves her, sit and talk with her when she wants him to, or ask her what's wrong when she appears to be feeling down in the dumps.

When the session ends, James has a list of things to do in the coming week. He will not correct his wife. He will give her one compliment and do one nice thing for her each day. And he will write a list of fifty things he likes about *himself* and bring it to our next session. He thinks the list is ridiculous but agrees to do it.

Because James is a Corrector, I know that not only is he too critical of his wife, but he's entirely too critical of himself. That's why I want him to learn to focus on the things he likes about himself as well as on what he likes about his wife. Unless he changes his view of the world and replaces his everyday negative thoughts with more positive ones, he's not going to be able to stop being critical.

I warn James that his wife also may be hooked on those critical remarks he gives her (even though she complains about them) because critical remarks are a form of recognition.

As I hand James an appointment card for the following week, I feel optimistic but know he has much work ahead of him.

One of the things that is interesting is that Kate and Richard and

James all knew to some degree what they could do differently to make their marriages better. And yet, none of them did what needed to be done. The reason they didn't make the changes on their own is because they discounted* what they knew. In addition, all of them kept expecting their spouses to change in order to make the marriage better. Once they understood that they *alone* could make the difference and they started to change their own behavior, their marriages would improve.

WHICH OF YOUR BEHAVIORS WOULD *YOUR* MATE CHANGE?

When you think about your own marriage, I suspect, there are things you know you could do that would make your relationship better. Perhaps your mate hates it when you curse, or when you don't put away your toothbrush, or when every once in a while you take the liberty and borrow *his* toothbrush. These behaviors would be relatively easy to change. And, believe it or not, they would definitely make a difference in how your spouse feels about you.

So come on. 'Fess up. What are some of the things *you* do that your mate finds irritating? Jot down two things he or she would change about you.

1. _____

2. _____

Behaviors That Make a Difference

If you're stuck and can't seem to come up with anything your spouse would want you to do differently, read over the following list. The items on this list seem to come up over and over when I do counseling. And although every marriage is unique, some common elements seem to be a part of all relationships. As you read over the list, put a check mark by those items that you *know* would improve your marriage.

☐ Say thank you more often.
☐ Be more courteous.
☐ Give more compliments.

- [ ] Look up and recognize him when he comes into the room.
- [ ] Be more affectionate.
- [ ] Tell her she's pretty.
- [ ] Say "I love you."
- [ ] Approach him sexually.
- [ ] Remember her birthday and Valentine's Day.
- [ ] Be willing to have sex more frequently.
- [ ] Stop criticizing him in public.
- [ ] Take the time to talk to him.
- [ ] Make the time to do fun things together.
- [ ] Keep a running balance in the checkbook.
- [ ] Cut down on drinking.
- [ ] Stop name calling.
- [ ] Stay on the budget.
- [ ] Help more with the children.
- [ ] Pick up after myself.
- [ ] Bring her little surprises.
- [ ] Flush the toilet.
- [ ] Stop getting so angry and escalating problems.
- [ ] Be on time or call if I'm going to be late.
- [ ] Tell him how I feel about something.
- [ ] Stick to the issue when we fight.
- [ ] Be willing to take turns going to the grocery store and the cleaners.
- [ ] Stop belching in front of her.
- [ ] Wash up my dirty dishes.
- [ ] Make the bed in the morning.
- [ ] Don't let the dog in with muddy feet.
- [ ] Take turns changing the cat litter.
- [ ] Don't leave him with an empty gas tank.
- [ ] Put away the hair drier when I'm done using it.
- [ ] Throw my junk mail away.
- [ ] Pick up the paper after I've read it.
- [ ] Do what I say I'm going to do (repair the screen door, contact a financial planner, etc.).

As you can see, a lot of the items on this list wouldn't be that difficult to do, but each item takes thought, particularly if you haven't been doing it in the past. Also, when you undertake something new, you're working against old habits and old patterns of behavior. So you have to make that extra effort.

Charlie's and Donna's "Do Differently" Lists

One man I was seeing in therapy came up with the following list of things he was willing to do to start the ball rolling in the right direction to make his marriage better.

1. I'll make her coffee in the morning and take it to her.
2. I'll initiate two conversations a day.
3. I'll give her some hugs.

Charlie was passive in his marriage. What he needed to do differently was be more active, initiate things, and take better care of his wife. After he made his list, I suggested that he also decide how many hugs he was going to give his wife each day. Initially he was hesitant to commit to exactly how many hugs. I have found, however, that the more specific people are, the more likely they are to take their list seriously and thus get the job done. It's a little like having a deadline on the job. Charlie decided on three hugs a day.

Donna, another woman I worked with who was feeling overwhelmed with everything she had to do in her marriage, made the following list:

1. I'm going to stop complaining about everything I have to do.
2. I'm going to stop picking up the slack and doing the chores my husband has agreed to do.
3. I'm going to initiate one fun thing for us to do each week and then actually do it with him.

In some marriages a partner will need to do *more* things in the relationship to make it better, as with Charlie, who was passive, and Richard, who did what he darn well pleased. In other marriages a spouse will need to *stop* doing something he is doing, as with James, who needed to stop criticizing his wife. And, in other marriages, a spouse actually needs to do *less* in the relationship, as in the cases of Donna and Kate, who took care of their husbands too well and needed to bring more of a balance to their marriages.

Your "Do Differently" List

Now it's your turn. Think of the things you are willing to do differently in your marriage to start moving it in the right direction.

Don't make the items on your list too difficult at first, because you'll be less likely to follow through. Also, take the time to write your list in the space provided; this will help you make the commitment.

1. _____

2. _____

3. _____

You also might put a copy of this list in a place where you'll see it every day. You can put it in your underwear drawer, tape it to the inside of the medicine cabinet, or attach it to the sun visor in your car. Then vow that no matter what, you will keep doing the things on your list. Remember, living Happily Ever After depends on it.

GIVE IT A CHANCE

Sometimes a person will ask me, "How long am I expected to keep this list?" The answer is forever if you plan to have a good marriage. But right now make the commitment to keep to your list for four weeks. That will get things moving along in the right direction and help you start "feeling" the benefits of keeping your list. By the end of the fourth week, keeping it will be second nature. If your spouse acts irritable or nasty in that period (and he or she probably will; it's human), do your list anyway. After all, if your boss acts obnoxious, you don't stop working; and if your child misbehaves, you don't stop parenting.

Occasionally a person also will say, "How come *I* have to make all the changes? What about my spouse? He's the one that causes most of the problems in our marriage. He's the one who's always losing his temper or pouting or drinking too much." That may be true, but you have an investment in making the marriage better. So you change, and he'll change. It may take a few months, but don't worry—he'll change.

It's also a good idea to think through how you might sabotage yourself and not keep your list. For example, let's suppose you've decided to come home on time. For four nights you make the extra effort and get home on time, and your wife doesn't say anything about your changed behavior. Or when you do come home, she's on the telephone with one of her friends, and she doesn't give you the time of day. Don't use her behavior as your excuse to stop following your list. Come home on time anyway; she'll eventually start recognizing that you are on time. If she doesn't, and you have kept your list for two or three weeks, you can always say something to her such as, "I've been coming home on time because I know that's what you want. So when I come home, how about the two of us taking a short walk or sitting on the porch and talking?"

If you're one of those Caretaker spouses (the ones who try to do everything in the relationship), and you've decided to do less, be careful not to sabotage yourself by saying that you can do it faster or better than your spouse. Of course you could be more efficient— you've had a lot of practice. But unless you stop trying to do everything, your spouse will never learn. Also remember that "I can do it better" is simply an excuse to get back into the Caretaker position and take over once again.

Sometimes when I give people this assignment, they think it's too easy or too pat or that it doesn't deal with the underlying dynamics of a relationship. Or they ask, "How could doing three things differently each day possibly have an impact on a marriage that has been lousy for sixteen years?"

To answer this question, let me tell you about Charlie, the man who decided to make his wife coffee in the morning, initiate two conversations a day, and give three hugs a day.

Charlie came into marriage counseling because his wife had given him an ultimatum that basically said, "Either you change or I'm leaving." What Charlie needed to work on in therapy was his poor self-image. He also lacked motivation both at home and at the office. At home he rarely did anything but read the newspaper or watch television. He didn't initiate sex, social plans, or conversation. Nor did he take responsibility on his own and fix anything around the house. When I asked him if there was anything he did initiate, he laughed a little and said, "Going fishing." He would go fishing with a friend about every two months.

His work record was equally bad. He missed deadlines, often arrived late, and at the time he came to counseling, his job was in jeopardy because of poor performance.

By our second session two weeks later, however, he was feeling better about his life. He had followed his list religiously and was feeling good just because he had kept it. This was an accomplishment in itself. He had also started working out with his son's weights in the basement and had lost seven pounds. And he had initiated sex three times. He was glowing. His wife, in response to his new behavior, was definitely feeling better about the relationship.

On one hand, the list didn't directly address the underlying issues of Charlie's passivity and poor self-image. But on the other hand, the list was attacking and chipping away at these very issues. As Charlie did more in the relationship, he was starting to change his passive position and become more active. And this was changing his view of himself. At the same time, his wife was giving him praise for "doing," which also was helping Charlie see himself more favorably.

Keeping your Do Differently List every day *will* make an impact on you and your marriage. And if you still doubt it, try it for four weeks. You'll see.

SECRET GAME PLANS

Another session in marriage counseling involves figuring out some of the Secret Game Plans[1] that you and your partner have established through the years. Every marriage has them, and although some promote a healthy relationship, others can be destructive and lead to any number of marital problems.

THE SECRETS BEHIND THE GAME PLANS

Generally when people think in terms of a game plan in their marriage, they are thinking of certain things they have consciously decided to do together to reach a particular goal. One couple decides that they are going to save an additional amount of money each month for the next two years so they can make a down payment on a house. Another couple decides that the wife will work outside the home a certain period of time, and all her money will go into savings for the children's education.

While they might discuss these game plans openly, couples also set up some *Secret* Game Plans that they will follow throughout their marriage. When she puts on a special nightgown, he "knows" that she plans to have sex that night. When he calls to say he is going to stop on his way home to pick up a couple of steaks, she "knows" that he wants to spend the evening talking about what's going on at work.

These Secret Game Plans have become an accepted but unspoken part of the marriage. What's going to happen doesn't need to be discussed; it just occurs because the couple has done it over and over. They have a covert agreement that this is the way it's going to be done. When I do this, you'll do that. When you say this, I'll say that. When you do this, I'll do that.

While some Secret Game Plans actually add to the closeness and camaraderie that a husband and wife feel in the marriage, others end in bad feelings and cause any number of problems in the relationship. And these are the Game Plans that you especially will want to be aware of in your marriage.

In order to identify your Secret Game Plan, all you need to do is ask yourself *what you fight about* and *how the fight proceeds*. To help you understand this, I called several of my friends when I was in the process of writing this chapter and I asked them what they fought about in their marriages.

The Who-Does-What Fight

When I asked Mary Lou, she said without hesitation, "Paul and I fight about chores. Or rather, I fight about chores with Paul."

Their disagreement usually begins with Mary Lou starting to feel overburdened with everything there is to do. She makes a few choice comments to Paul about how much she has to do around the house. She asks why everything is her responsibility, because she also works a full-time job and brings in a paycheck.

After a few such comments, Paul knows that he's headed for the doghouse, so he'll say something like, "Well, what do you want me to do?" This makes her even more furious because she thinks he should know what needs to be done; after all, he lives in the house, too.

So she says, "If I have to tell you what needs to be done, never mind!" At this point he disappears upstairs to work on his computer, while she storms around the house, infuriated at him and feeling like a victim.

The worst thing is that this couple has this fight at least two or three times a month. It is their favorite Secret Game Plan.

The Anything-Will-Kill-You-These-Days Fight

When I asked another friend what she and her husband fight about, she said, "Oh, that's easy. We fight about Bob's smoking." She'll hear or read something about cigarettes being detrimental to one's health, and will get all revved up and go on a campaign to convince her husband to quit smoking. But no matter what she says, he tells her that he's different. After all, his grandfather smoked and lived to be in his eighties; anything will kill you these days, even water; and you've got to die of something.

She'll then try another tactic, such as telling him that his smoking is not attractive and it turns her off. He tells her that it's one of his pleasures, he works hard, and how could she deny him? She'll suggest that he try cutting back on his smoking because she wants him around after the children are grown. And maybe he could smoke only every other day. Or what about smoking only right after a meal?

By this time her husband is angry with her, and the rest of the evening is spent with him pouting and her feeling guilty. She feels terrible because she knows she'll never get anywhere with this subject; she's not going to win, and there's going to be no compromising. But about once a month she can't seem to resist reenacting this Secret Game Plan.

The Who-Says-"Hi"-First Fight

My husband and I used to fight about who said "Hi" first. When he came in from work and I was home before him, I would walk over to him, give him a kiss on the cheek, and say, "Hi, honey, how are you?"

But when I came in from work and he was already there, he still waited for me to come over to him, give him a peck on the cheek, and be the first to say, "Hi, honey." In fact, he even turned his cheek so I could kiss him. What I wanted was for him to greet me, not for me to always have to greet him. I wanted to be recognized and taken care of, and not to always have to take care of him.

Occasionally we still find ourselves playing a variation of this game when he comes home from a business trip. He walks into the house and says, "Did you miss me?" Of course, when he says this, I instantly feel annoyed because what I want is for him to focus on me and say he missed *me*. If I say I missed him, he gets my attention instead of my getting his. He gets taken care of instead of me. Ideally what we both should do is say how we missed each other.

What continually fascinates me is that all of us know the issues that we fight about, and we can all go back and recount step by step what happens in the argument. The steps, of course, are simply a part of our Secret Game Plan.

SIX QUESTIONS TO DETERMINE YOUR DESTRUCTIVE SECRET GAME PLAN

When I see a couple in counseling and they start to tell me about a disagreement they've had, I'll often suggest that we look at their Game Plan, which involves answering six questions. After answering these questions, it's easy for us to go back and figure out at what step each of them could have changed their behavior and avoided the bad feelings that both experienced at the end of their Secret Game Plan.

The six questions that will help you discover your Secret Game Plan are:

1. **What happens over and over in your relationship that causes bad feelings?** *(What do you fight about most frequently?)*

2. **How does the whole thing start?** *(Who does or says what first?)*

3. **Then what happens?** *(What do you or your spouse do or say in response?)*

4. **What happens next?** *(What do you do or what does your mate do in response?)*

5. **How does it all end?** *(What do you or your spouse do or say to end the fight?)*

6. **How do you feel afterward?** *(Are you mad, sad, scared?)*

Keep in mind that it doesn't matter who initiates the Game Plan because we all start the ball rolling from time to time. The important thing to remember is that either one of you can stop the game before its hurtful conclusion.

Mary Lou's Game Plan

Now let's look at a step-by-step example to show how the Game Plan works. Let's take the fight that Mary Lou and Paul are forever having over chores. Here's how Mary Lou answered the six Game Plan questions.

1. **What happens over and over in your relationship that causes bad feelings?**
   "Paul and I always seem to get into it over the fact that he doesn't help around the house."

2. **How does the whole thing start?**
   "I'm busy doing something and feeling overworked, while Paul's sitting there on the sofa reading or watching television. So I start complaining—loud enough so Paul can hear me—about how much I have to do, insinuating how he isn't doing anything."

3. **Then what happens?**
   "After a few choice comments from me, Paul usually volunteers to help. He does this by asking me what I want him to do."

4. **What happens next?**
   "I say that if I have to *tell* him what needs to be done, just forget it. Never mind!"

5. **How does it all end?**
   "He goes off to do his own thing because I've told him to forget it, while I'm stuck doing all the chores."

6. **How do you feel afterward?**
   "I'm plenty mad at the fact that he doesn't help me more. After all, why is everything my responsibility?"

When Mary Lou looks at their Secret Game Plan, she finds that she could change the whole situation if she did something differently at Step 2 or Step 4. At Step 2, instead of complaining about how Paul never seems to help her, she could say, "I'd like it if you'd help me with the chores, Paul."

Let's assume, however, that Mary Lou gets into the game and initially doesn't ask Paul for help, but instead mumbles and grumbles. At Step 4 she could still save the situation by telling her husband what he could do once he asks. Even though at this point Mary Lou is the one who has to take major responsibility and point out exactly what chores Paul should do, she's still ahead because she gets help with the chores. Also, in the long run, there's a possibility that her husband will begin to see what needs to be done without being told. When she simply tells him, "Never mind," she's setting it up for him "never" to be helpful.

The goal for Mary Lou and Paul is for each to pitch in and get the chores done together. In this way both of them take responsibility.

The Checkbook Fight

Another couple used to start their Secret Game Plan when the husband, Bob, balanced the checkbook.

Bob would be working on the checkbook, and Alice would come in and say, "Hi, dear. How's it going?" Still looking at his figures, he would respond, "This checkbook doesn't balance." That's all she needed to hear.

Faithfully taking her cue, she would say, "Well, I didn't make the mistake." And he would take his turn and reply, "I didn't say anything about you making a mistake." Then she would counter with, "You know darn well you think I made it." At this point Alice would huff out of the room and think, "He must think he's perfect," while Bob would sit there thinking, "What's the problem?"

Every few months this couple went through this routine when Bob balanced the checkbook. They were amazed when I asked them the Game Plan questions and they could see step by step what they were doing.

Alice's Position:

Here's how the wife answered the six Game Plan questions.

1. **What happens over and over in your relationship that causes bad feelings?**
   "We fight about the checkbook."

2. **How does the whole thing start?**
   "My husband tells me it doesn't balance."

3. **Then what happens?**
   "I tell him he's accusing me of messing up the checkbook."

4. **What happens next?**
   "He denies that's what he's doing."

5. **How does it all end?**
   "I leave the room feeling put down and believing that somehow he thinks I'm stupid."

6. **How do you feel afterward?**
   "I feel indignant . . . mad. And sad that our evening has ended with a fight."

Looking at the answers, you can see that Alice could have changed her behavior at Step 3 or Step 5. At Step 3, instead of telling Bob that he was accusing her of messing up the checkbook, she could say, "What seems to be the problem?" or, "Is there anything I can do to help you figure it out?" At Step 5, instead of leaving the room in a huff, she could decide not to continue to fight and then offer to lend a hand.

Bob's Position:

Here's how the husband answered the same questions.

1. **What happens over and over in your relationship that causes bad feelings?**
   "Every time I balance the checkbook, we wind up in a fight."

2. **How does the whole thing start?**
   "My wife asks me how it's going, and I tell her the checkbook doesn't balance."

3. **Then what happens?**
   "She immediately gets irritated and says I'm accusing her of making the mistake."

4. **What happens next?**
   "I deny that's what I'm saying."

5. **How does it all end?**
   "She huffs out of the room, and I sit there wondering how the whole thing started. I think her behavior is a little ridiculous. I also continue to work on balancing the checkbook."

6. **How do you feel afterward?**
"I feel mad because I think she's unreasonable, and I also feel sad because the evening is ruined."

Looking at this Game Plan, it's apparent that Bob could have changed his behavior at Step 2 or Step 4. Instead of saying at Step 2 that the checkbook doesn't balance, he could say, "I've run into a snag, but with any luck I'll figure it out." At Step 4, instead of denying that he's accusing Alice of making a mistake, he could say, "I don't know who made the mistake. The real problem is that I absolutely hate balancing the checkbook. And I'm sorry that I sound annoyed with you."

No matter what steps were handled differently, each of them could have avoided feeling irritated and sad, and the bad evening that followed.

The Orange-Juice Fight

One couple I saw in marriage counseling fought about, of all things, orange juice. Here's their unique scenario.

Bill would get up in the morning and say, "Will you have time to stop for my orange juice today?" Ann would reply, "Sure, I'll get it." Then that night, as they were getting into bed, he would say, "Did you get my orange juice?" To which she would respond, "I got too busy. And besides, if it's so darn important that you have orange juice every morning, pick up your own!" Then he would come back with, "I would have if you hadn't told me you were going to get it."

He would turn out the bedroom light at that point, and the two of them would lie there stiff as boards, feeling furious at each other. Bill would think to himself, "After all I do for her, and I can't even count on her for orange juice." Ann, of course, would be thinking to herself, "Why can't he take care of himself for once and get his own orange juice?"

Bill's Position:

Bill's answers to the six Game Plan questions make it unquestionably clear how rapidly things can move along to cause a breakdown in a relationship.

1. **What happens over and over in your relationship that causes bad feelings?**
   "My wife says she'll do something like stop and get my orange juice, and then she doesn't."

2. **How does the whole thing start?**
   "I ask her if she can pick up some orange juice."

3. **Then what happens?**
   "She says okay."

4. **What happens next?**
   "That night I ask her if she got my orange juice."

5. **How does it all end?**
   "She tells me she didn't get the juice and that if it was that important, I should have stopped myself."

6. **How do you feel afterward?**
   "I feel mad that I can't count on her and also sad that she doesn't seem to care enough to make one lousy stop."

It's clear that this husband could have averted or changed this destructive Game Plan at Step 2. Instead of asking Ann to get his orange juice, he could have taken responsibility and done it himself, since past experience has shown that Ann hasn't been dependable in carrying out this task. If he insisted, however, on testing fate again and asking Ann to get the juice, he needed to be prepared in advance for a possible disappointment.

Ann's Position:

Ann, on the other hand, also had some options. At Step 3 she could have told Bill that she wouldn't be able to stop for the juice or that she would get it if she had time, thus indicating that she might not pick up the juice. She also could have said that she would get the juice and then, no matter what, followed through.

Either Bill or Ann could have changed their Secret Game Plan without too much difficulty. They didn't, however, because it provided them with too many benefits, as you'll start to see in the following chapters.

The After-the-Party Fight

Here's another Game Plan a couple discovered using the six questions. In this Secret Game Plan, Mary and Dave always fought after a party. At the party the husband would take a potshot at his wife. She, of course, would immediately feel irritated, but because she believed it was inappropriate to cause a scene in public, she would pretend that she hadn't heard the comment.

Mary's Position:

1. **What happens over and over in your relationship that causes bad feelings?**
   "We fight on the way home from parties."

2. **How does the whole thing start?**
   "While we're at the party, my husband usually says something derogatory about me, like how I forgot to do something . . . something that implies I'm stupid."

3. **Then what happens?**
   "I don't say anything at that time because I don't think people should fight in public. But when we get in the car, I let him have it with both barrels."

4. **What happens next?**
   "He denies that he meant to hurt me, or he says that I'm too sensitive."

5. **How does it all end?**
   "We're both quiet the rest of the way home. And, of course, there's no further communication or sex that night."

6. **How do you feel afterward?**
   "Usually discouraged. And also kind of sad, because he keeps doing something that hurts me and then he denies that he meant it."

In this plan, Mary could change at Step 3 or Step 5. At Step 3, while at the party, instead of remaining silent when Dave takes a potshot at her, she could say, "Oh, come on, Dave." A statement like this wouldn't cause a scene, but it would certainly call attention to

Dave's inappropriate remark. Also, if she deals with her husband's comment right then and there, her bad feelings are more likely to dissipate by the time they leave the party. Mary also could decide not to respond to her husband's comment on the way home but instead bring up the issue the following day, when she cools down.

At Step 5 she could talk with Dave instead of remaining quiet. And she could even initiate sex when they get home.

Dave's Position:

Dave also could change this destructive Game Plan. He could refrain from taking a potshot at Mary at the party. Or, if he inadvertently does make a crack and hears himself doing it, he could apologize right there at the party or when they reach the car. Or, at the very least, he should apologize when Mary confronts him about his behavior. Any one of these changes on Dave's part would result in a more pleasant ending to the evening.

IDENTIFYING YOUR DESTRUCTIVE SECRET GAME PLAN

Now it's time for you to get in touch with one of your Secret Game Plans. I suspect that as you answer the questions, you'll be amazed at how well you know what you fight about and how the fight proceeds. For this exercise I suggest that you take the time to write down your answers, since you'll be referring back to them.

1. **What happens over and over in your relationship that causes bad feelings?**
   (What do you fight about most frequently?)

   _____

2. **How does the whole thing start?** *(Who does or says what first?)*

   _____

3. **Then what happens?** *(What do you or your spouse do or say in response?)*

_____

4. **What happens next?** *(What do you do or what does your mate do in response?)*

_____

5. **How does it all end?** *(What do you or your spouse do or say to end the fight?)*

_____

6. **How do you feel afterward?** *(Are you mad, sad, scared?)*

_____

   Now go back and look at your answers and decide at which step or steps you might handle things differently in the future.

   By using the six Game Plan questions, you can see how a particular game gets started and how it proceeds step by step. You can also see that it doesn't make any difference who starts the game, because either you or your spouse can turn things around by responding differently. This is one of the best things about identifying your Secret Game Plan; you don't have to wait for your partner to change. If you change, your relationship will get better.

COMMUNICATION

WHAT ARE YOU REALLY SAYING?

When I'm seeing someone in my office, one thing I continually focus on is how the person communicates. If he doesn't look at me, I'll say, "How about looking at me." If he interrupts me, I might say, "You cut me off before I finished my sentence." Or if he doesn't answer a question, I might say, "You didn't answer my question," or, "You just 'switched the issue.' "*

If I'm working with a couple, more information is available, and I'm able to observe firsthand how they interact with each other as well as with me. For instance, the husband might say something that suggests covertly that his wife is stupid, or he calls her "honey" while he's busy putting her down. The wife might be talking to her husband and looking at the floor or out the window, or she says, "Why don't you . . . ," implying of course what he should be doing.

I point out these destructive behaviors by saying, "Hold on. How can you say that differently?" or, "Say that again but this time take out the sarcasm," or, "Stop. Tilt. Oops, do it again."

I also have about three dozen Nerf® balls* lying around the office, and when someone goofs, I "nerf" them—that is, I throw a Nerf ball at them as a way to call their attention to the fact that they have messed up. When a person is nerfed,* he usually responds with laughter, which indicates to me that he or she understands the confrontation. Of course, they have the same option, and when I goof, they nerf me. I've been

32

using this technique for many years, and I've found that nerfing a person helps take some of the sting out of a confrontation and also encourages people not to take their mistake so seriously.

When I first see someone for counseling, I'll probably point out fifteen or twenty communication stoppers during the session. So initially we spend about a third of the time discussing ways that the person actually blocks communication. I put a high priority on the way people talk with each other, because communication errors cause a lot of trouble in a marriage; and every error creates just one more barrier to closeness in a marriage. Also, every error has the possibility of setting in motion some psychological game.

As you read through the examples, you undoubtedly will see communication errors that you and your spouse are in the habit of making. Once you're able to identify these errors, you can start to change the way you communicate, and as you change, your marriage will get better.

Downplaying Feelings

One way to stop communication is to downplay your spouse's feelings. For instance, when the wife says, "I feel crummy today," and her husband responds, "You'll feel better tomorrow," or, "Everybody is depressed sometime," he's downplaying her feelings.

Unfortunately, this husband is sending the covert message,* "Go away. I don't want to talk about your crummy day." What's sad is that this guy doesn't even know if his wife is feeling emotionally crummy or physically crummy or if something specific happened that day to cause her to feel this way.

One husband I saw in therapy downplayed his wife's feelings in the following manner.

Joan, the wife, was on a diet, and it seemed this time she was finally going to lose the weight she had put on shortly after her marriage. At the time she had lost about thirty pounds. Then one Saturday morning Joan's husband, Rick, went out for a paper. Besides bringing home the paper, he brought home a box of doughnuts. Joan was beside herself. She responded to the doughnuts by saying, "Rick, I'm furious at you for bringing home those doughnuts. I'm dieting!" Rick replied, "Now don't go and get all mad and ruin the day."

In this situation Rick discounted Joan's dieting, and then he proceeded to downplay her feelings when he suggested to Joan that her anger would ruin the day. Certainly Rick shouldn't have brought the doughnuts home in the first place. But he still could have redeemed himself. After he was confronted by Joan, he could have said, "You're right, I'm sorry. I can see that bringing home doughnuts wasn't very considerate."

The classic example of downplaying feelings is when the wife says, "I get the feeling that you don't care about me anymore." And the husband responds, "You know I care about you." Two minutes later the wife says, "Well, I don't think you do."

At this point you would think the husband would take a different approach, but once again he tries to reassure his wife by saying, "Come on, I said I cared." This comment only serves to validate his wife's perception that he doesn't care. If he does care, why does he sound annoyed? Why doesn't he ask what she means when she says, "I don't think you care"?

This husband needs to handle the situation differently and ask, "Why don't you think I care?" This question would serve to open things up. Or he could say, "Is there anything I can do to show you that I care?" When he finds out why his wife feels uncared for or what he can do to show her he cares, he can start making the appropriate changes in his behavior. If he doesn't have the information, however, he can't change.

The wife, too, could communicate more clearly. She could say, "Sometimes I think you don't care because you ask me about my day, and before I have a chance to answer you, you're looking through the mail or you're reading the newspaper."

Note again the important lesson here: *Either spouse has the power to change things around.*

Another classic is the wife who says to her husband, "I feel so hurt," and her husband says, "Don't feel hurt." Here he not only downplays her feeling but in addition he tells her not to feel. If he is unclear about why she feels hurt, he might say, "Why are you feeling hurt?" If he already knows the event that has precipitated this feeling, he might say, "Is there anything I can do that will help you feel less hurt?"

I had one woman tell me that she walked into the house crying. She had been to an aerobics class and found she couldn't keep pace with the class. She felt really bad about herself and the fact that she wasn't in the kind of shape she had been when she was younger. When she told her husband why she was crying, he laughed and said,

"You've got to be kidding. I thought somebody had died." Clearly he was sending her the message "Don't feel." How much better it would have been had he put his arm around her and said, "It's really tough when you initially start to exercise. But you'll get back in shape. It'll just take some time."

Another unfortunate consequence that occurs when your feelings have been downplayed is that you often experience even more feelings as you try to reexplain your position to your mate.

For example, a husband tells his wife that he feels irritated because she's always correcting him in front of their friends. Instead of acknowledging his feelings and apologizing for her behavior, she defends herself and tells him it's important she set the record straight so he doesn't look foolish. So again he tells her how he feels, but this time he tells her with more irritation in his voice.

If after reading these examples you have become aware that you downplay your spouse's feelings, you might find the following points helpful.

1. If your spouse says that she feels sad, worried, scared, overworked, delighted, irritable, or happy, find out why she feels that way. Ask questions, and make the decision that you won't dismiss how your spouse feels.

2. If your spouse tells you something and then repeats the exact same thing again, you can bet she didn't get the response she wanted from you the first time. So don't give her the same answer the second time, since this only closes off communication further.

3. If it's your mate who downplays your feelings, point this out. You might say, "When I tell you how I feel and you tell me it will all be better in the morning, I get the idea that you don't want me to bother you. And then I feel even worse."

If feelings are being downplayed, either one of you can correct the situation and make the relationship better.

Problem Solving Too Quickly

Another communication blocker that couples habitually use is trying to solve their spouse's problem too quickly instead of simply listening.

A classic example is the fellow who comes home from work and says, "I'm exhausted. I must have had twenty phone calls today plus the usual. And everybody expects immediate action." To which his wife says, "Why don't you quit that job? It's not worth the hassle."

This husband now has two problems. Not only does he feel wrung out from the day's events, but now he must defend his job. All this husband needed was to be able to complain a little, get some sympathy, and perhaps play a few rounds of Ain't-It-Awful[*1] (a back-and-forth repartee about how difficult life can be).

Here's another example of a spouse trying to solve the problem too quickly. Sally says to Tim, "If I get all the presents bought before Christmas, it will be a miracle." And Tim says, "Why don't you just give everybody money and be done with it?"

Sally probably was looking for some recognition for the time she spent on Christmas shopping, or maybe she covertly was asking for some help. Instead her husband gave her a quick solution that discounted the shopping she had already done. What Tim might have said is, "Why don't you think you'll get it finished?" This recognizes what Sally has said and also expresses interest.

Everyone needs time to talk, to complain, to moan and groan, and to be listened to. So be careful that you give your spouse this kind of time.

Giving Pat Answers

Another communication stopper that couples use is pat answers. Such statements as "It'll all work out," "Don't worry, you'll get over it," "What can you expect?" and "It'll be okay" all fall into the pat answer category. Because these words are used so often in everyday conversation, they lose their meaning and rarely provide comfort.

If your wife tells you that she's not getting along with someone at the office, don't tell her, "It'll all work out." Instead, ask her why she's not getting along or what she thinks the problem is. If your husband says he's feeling pressure on his job, don't tell him he'll see things differently the next day. Open up the communication and ask him what's going on.

Since pat answers are part of everyone's conversation, it's important to be aware of the ones you're most likely to use. Once you're aware of them, you'll be less apt to use them in the future. So jot down two of your favorites.

1. _____

2. _____

Now over the next few weeks monitor what you say, and see if you can get rid of these rather boring, overworked, and unsupportive comments.

Asking Closed-Ended Questions

Couples also block communication by asking closed-ended questions. Such questions can be answered with a yes or no, or a word or two. If Marsha asks Rob, "Did your meeting go well?" she will most likely get a yes-or-no answer. If instead she says, "What happened at the meeting?" she's likely to get more information. And she's also more likely to convey that she's interested in her husband's day.

Here are some closed-ended questions that have been made into open-ended ones:

- _"Did you have fun at bridge club last night?"_ **becomes** "What did you think of bridge?"

- _"Are you going to work Saturday?"_ **becomes** "What are your plans on Saturday?"

- _"Do you want to go out this weekend?"_ **becomes** "What would you like to do this weekend?"

Now you try it. Change these closed-ended questions to open-ended ones:

- _"Did you like the book?"_ **becomes** _____

- _"Was the movie good?"_ **becomes** _____

- _"Did you get a lot done today?"_ **becomes** _____

Some possible answers are:

"What did you think of the book?"

"What did you think of the movie?"

"What did you get done today?"

Asking Questions with a Hidden Agenda

One of the most destructive communication errors that couples make is asking a question with a hidden agenda, or a secret message. Questions that start with "Don't you think . . . ," "Wouldn't you agree . . . ," and "Why don't you . . ." often contain hidden agendas.

When your spouse introduces a question with "Don't you think," you're being told what to think. When your spouse begins with "Wouldn't you agree," you're being primed to agree. And when your spouse starts a question with "Why don't you," you're being told what to do.

For several years I did a spot on television called *Psychologically Speaking.* I would answer a question sent in by a viewer, and then the television personality and I would discuss the subject. As we were discussing anger one day, the fellow said, "Say, Doris, don't you think it's okay to scream at your wife *every* once in a while?" I said, "No, I don't think screaming serves any good purpose. In fact, it's a way to not deal with the issue." So again he asked, "But don't you think if you scream, it sometimes gets to the bottom of things?" Again I ducked his hidden agenda and said, "I think you can get to the bottom of things without screaming." And *again* he asked, "But isn't screaming a good way to clear the air?" With that question I started laughing and said, "I bet you scream at your wife."

The laughter from the cameramen in the television studio was so loud that I was told you could hear it on the television sets at home. I later found out that this man used to get into screaming matches with his wife over the telephone, and the people at the station apparently had heard some of these fights. Clearly this fellow wanted to be told that screaming at his wife was all right, and with each question he was setting me up to agree with him.

Many questions have hidden agendas. The question "Don't you think we ought to put in an appearance?" contains the hidden agenda "We should put in an appearance." "Isn't this restaurant a little expensive?" contains the hidden agenda "I think this restaurant is expensive." And "Why did you do that?" usually contains the hidden agenda "I don't think you should have done that."

The question "Don't you think that suit is a little outdated?" has several possible hidden agendas. The most obvious is, "Your suit is outdated." This spouse also might be saying, "Get yourself some new clothes," "You're a lousy dresser," or, "Stop wearing that suit around me."

A woman asked her husband the following question right as the three of us sat down to start our session: "Joe, do you like your hair cut that short?" Joe, a little annoyed, said, "Yeah. It's okay." The wife then asked me, "Do you like his hair cut that short?" I nerfed her and said, "Come on, Rose, you need to make a statement." She giggled and said, "Well, Joe, I don't like your hair that short."

Another hidden agenda is revealed by the couple going on vacation. On seeing her suitcases, the husband says to his wife, "You're taking all those?" This implies, of course, that she must be out of her mind for taking so many clothes. The wife certainly heard the hidden agenda, for she pouted the first four hours of their vacation.

One of my favorite stories is about a fellow who said to his wife, "I made myself the best tuna salad yesterday." To which she asked, "What did you put in it?" He replied, "I'll get you the recipe." And she said, "You used a recipe to make tuna salad?" The hidden agenda: "You dummy. No one uses a recipe for tuna salad."

Backseat drivers are notorious for asking questions with hidden agendas. Some favorites are, "Why are you taking the highway?", "Why are we in this lane?", and "What's the rush?" It doesn't take much thought to figure out the hidden agendas in these questions.

When you ask a question with a hidden agenda, your spouse hears the hidden agenda and often responds to the secret message.

When Rose asked Joe if he liked his haircut, Joe knew exactly what Rose was saying. Because Joe had a short fuse, I suspect that if I hadn't been there, Joe would have said something sarcastic, such as, "Since when are you concerned about how I look?" This comment would have been in response to Rose's hidden agenda. And soon Rose and Joe would have been fighting over who cares most about their appearance or what a jerk he was last week at her mother's birthday party.

As you can see, asking a question with a hidden agenda is often a setup to fight. Also, you're not taking responsibility for what you think or what you want, but instead you are trying to manipulate your partner to think as you think or to do what you want.

If you're the spouse on the receiving end of such a question, you can turn it around quite easily. When asked, "Don't you think we should make an appearance?" you can say, "Sounds like you think we should make an appearance." This statement pushes your mate to take responsibility for her opinion and say whether she thinks the two of you should put in an appearance.

If your spouse says, "Don't you think that suit is a bit outdated?" you can say, "Sounds as though you think my suit is outdated," or, "It seems like you want me to wear something else." Again, this puts the responsibility back on your mate.

"Not Owning" Your Statements

Often a spouse distances himself from his partner by using the pronouns "you" or "one" instead of the first-person "I." In the following two statements the only things that are different are the pronouns: "When *one* feels anxious *every* day of *one's* life, *one* has a hard time managing" versus "When *I* feel anxious *every* day of *my* life, *I* have a hard time managing." Most people would be more likely to respond to the second statement because it's more personal.

Here's another example: "When *you* think about the advances that technology will make over the next ten years, *you* feel a little overwhelmed" versus "When *I* think about the advances that technology will make over the next ten years, *I* feel a little overwhelmed."

Listen to yourself this week and see if you are guilty of this communication error. If so, you can correct it within a few days. Remember, using "you" or "one" is distancing and it weakens your statements, whereas "I" allows your mate to feel your involvement in what you're saying and makes your statement more powerful.

Stuck to Tar Baby

In some marriages one spouse will talk on and on, making it impossible for her mate to talk at all. The spouse who is forever talking is like Tar Baby—once she starts to talk, you can't stop her or get away from her. It's almost as if you're stuck to her, even though you're giving her clear signals that she needs to wind it up and give you the floor.

One woman I saw in marriage counseling was forever complaining that her husband never talked. But when he tried to talk, she just kept on talking. I literally used to get out of my chair and pretend I was going to put a Nerf ball in her mouth to get her to stop talking. Now she laughs about this, but for a long time it was a huge problem in their relationship.

If you recognize that *you* act like Tar Baby, remember you are inadvertently inviting your spouse not to talk to you and not to listen to you. Because if he gets into a conversation with you, it will quickly become a monologue, with you talking and him not listening. You can stop this behavior by making a pact with yourself that you will not go on for more than five sentences before you stop and let your husband respond with his comments. And be sure to count your sentences since most people who have this problem are not aware of how long they talk.

If your spouse has this habit, help her break it by pointing out how she talks on and on. You might say, "Come on, hon, bottom-line it." Or, "My turn." Unfortunately, some husbands allow their wives to go on talking while they sit there and take a trip in their head. This behavior is passive, and covertly it supports the wife's acting like Tar Baby.

Redefining or Switching the Issue

Another way couples get into trouble is by redefining* or changing the topic of conversation. Another name for redefining is switching the issue. They change what's being discussed and introduce a new topic without first addressing the issue at hand.

Here's a marital classic that you'll probably recognize immediately:

George: Your parents were certainly in a bad mood tonight.

Grace: Well, I've also seen your parents at each other's throats.

George: Ummm . . . At least we don't have anyone who comes to a family dinner drunk.

Here Grace shifts from an observation that George has made about *her* parents to an observation about *his* parents. And George shifts from his parents to comparing relatives. At this rate of exchange, it's predictable that George and Grace will be in an uproar in no time at all.

Here's another switching-the-issue exchange:

Ann: I think we need to sit down and go over our budget. With
      the bank note coming due on the house and Peter going
      to college next year, I think we're going to have to start
      saving more money.

Bob: If we could just get our charges paid off.

In this conversation Bob completely ignores what Ann has said
about the budget and instead switches to his own issue, paying off the
charge cards.

Two of my favorite redefinitions came within minutes of each
other during a marriage counseling session. The wife said to her husband, "You need to recognize that I have feelings, too, and that what
you say sometimes hurts." To which he said, "You're too sensitive."
Later in the session he said, "I think the problem is that you always
focus on the bad things in our marriage." And she replied, "You have
selective hearing." Obviously both were master redefiners. And because they had this technique down so well, they had trouble discussing
anything. A minute rarely went by when I wasn't nerfing one of them
for redefining the issue.

I'm sure you've had the experience of trying to reconstruct an
argument only to find that you can't even remember how the whole
thing started. You know that chores were an issue, and you remember
there was some discussion about money and when he was going to
lose weight. And you also recall bringing up that he needed to get
some better clothes and go to a different barber, and you remember
that he said he hated the lounge chairs you picked out. But for the
life of you, you can't remember how the argument got started. The
reason: a great many redefinitions.

Of all communication errors, this one occurs most frequently in
relationships and is perhaps the hardest to spot because most people
simply don't hear the redefinition when it's occurring. All they know
is that they started talking about one thing, and soon they were on
an entirely different track. And they never did get a response to their
comment or an answer to their question.

People usually switch the issue because they feel uncomfortable
with what has been said. They change the subject, and in that way
don't have to deal with the original issue. Another reason people
redefine is because they feel criticized or attacked; so they go on the

defensive and introduce a different subject. No one is so adept at this technique as the couple who has been married a few years, because each knows the other's vulnerabilities.

The way to solve a redefinition problem is to stick with one issue during a discussion. If your spouse redefines, you can state, "That's not the issue." If you miss the redefinition and find that you're both off and running, you can still stop yourself, go back, and say, "Wait a minute. Let's start this thing all over again." Once you're adept at sticking to the issue, you'll find that your conversations will be a lot more satisfying, your arguments will be shorter and less hostile, and there will be more goodwill in your relationship, since you both will feel that you are being listened to.

Nonverbal Communication

Nonverbal communication in marriage is sometimes even more important than verbal communication. It plays a major role in the way couples let each other know what they are really thinking and feeling.

Although I'm always saying, "You can't read your spouse's mind," most of you can walk into a room and be pretty sure what kind of mood your mate is in. The longer you live with someone, the better able you are to subconsciously read that person, which in some ways adds to the comfortableness of the relationship.

As long as you are picking up on good vibes, you don't need to comment on the nonverbal communication that goes on in your relationship. In fact, sometimes it would take away from the intimacy that the two of you may be feeling at that moment.

Where couples get into trouble, however, is when the nonverbal message being sent isn't a positive one. For example, the wife says something, and her husband responds by opening his mouth, tilting back his head, and staring at the ceiling. She keeps talking, however, completely ignoring his nonverbal comment. Or they are sitting at the table, and she lets out a disgusted sigh. Instead of saying anything, however, he pretends he hasn't heard and continues to read the newspaper. Or the husband gets into bed and instantly his wife stiffens up her body, gives the covers a quick jerk, and turns away from him. And he says nothing.

Usually when a spouse is presented with these nonverbal comments, he has a pretty good idea what's being said. Instead of dealing with the nonverbal messages directly, however, a spouse will often take the easy way out (or so he thinks) by not commenting on the nonverbal comment. When his mate detects that she is being ignored, she often turns up the volume to force her spouse to pay attention to her.

Another inappropriate way that people deal with this type of communication is to ask their spouse what's wrong when they already have a good idea what the problem is. Unfortunately, this maneuver often sets the stage for them to receive a whole barrage of criticism.

A good way to handle a wrinkled brow, a turned-up nose, a pouty face, a low whistle, an audible huff, a penetrating glance—any negative nonverbal comment—is to reflect back what your spouse must be feeling. For example, to the wife who let out a disgusted sigh at the table, the husband might have said, "You must be feeling frustrated." If he has a good idea what she's frustrated about, he might say, "You must be feeling frustrated because I'm reading the newspaper and ignoring you." Chances are this will open up communication. The husband's willingness to take some responsibility for how his wife is feeling will help her feel less irritated, and they will be in a better position to talk things out.

Another nonverbal message that definitely calls for a comment is when your spouse is *saying* something that does not match up with what he is *doing*. If he is telling you he doesn't like the way you handled one of the children, and he is smiling, you should comment on his smile. You might say, "When you sit there and criticize me for the way I handled Tommy, and then you smile, I get the feeling you're enjoying the fact that I messed up, or you're getting some satisfaction out of correcting me."

Two good rules of thumb to follow regarding negative nonverbal communication: (1) If your spouse sends you a negative nonverbal message, don't ignore it and don't ask what's wrong if you have some idea what's wrong. Instead, comment on what your spouse may be feeling. (2) If your spouse is talking to you and his nonverbal behavior does not match up with the content of what he is saying, bring it to his attention.

If you're the spouse who uses negative nonverbals, such as shrugs, glares, and disgusted sighs, make a pact with yourself to take responsibility and *comment openly* on what you don't approve of instead of sending a negative nonverbal and thereby putting the burden on your mate to comment on it.

THE BIGGER PICTURE

One reason people make so many communication errors is because they are not taught to be good communicators. People rarely are told that they are downplaying feelings or asking a question with a hidden agenda. So they simply do not have the information about how to communicate effectively.

Another reason is that communication errors play a large part in helping a person carry out his life plan. For example, if a boy is taught not to get close to people, he is likely to give pat answers and downplay feelings to avoid closeness. Thus later in life, when his wife says, "Gee, I feel blue," he will respond, "Everyone feels blue some of the time." Clearly this statement is impersonal and distancing. If, on the other hand, he says, "How come? What seems to be the matter?" he is taking the risk that his wife may share something vulnerable about herself, which would certainly create the opportunity for getting closer, something he is afraid of experiencing.

When Margaret was a child, she was taught that what she had to say was not as important as what her brothers had to say. Further, she was told that if you couldn't say something nice, you shouldn't say anything at all. As a result of her childhood, Margaret grew up believing that what she had to say wasn't very important and now she hides what she thinks by asking questions with hidden agendas.

After a party, Margaret asks her husband, "Dear, don't you think your jokes were a little out of line last night?" and, "Dear, don't you think those pants you wore were a bit tight?" Clearly, Margaret thinks Dear's jokes were inappropriate and his pants too tight. She disguises what she thinks and hides her negative thoughts by calling her husband "dear" and asking a question with a hidden agenda.

Now perhaps you're thinking, "Well, if my communication errors support what I've learned in childhood, it won't matter if I know how to be a more effective communicator because I'll keep making these errors in spite of myself." The reality, however, is that if you force yourself to change the way you communicate, your spouse will respond differently to you. And in turn you will start to naturally feel and act differently toward your spouse.

Suppose you were taught not to get emotionally close to people. Through the years you have subconsciously followed this message by giving your spouse pat answers. Now, however, you respond to what your mate says to you by commenting on his feelings and asking how you can be helpful to him. He, in turn, will feel listened to and taken care of, and he will respond to you differently. Maybe he'll talk more with you or ask you about what's happening on your job. As the two of you start to talk more, you'll start to feel closer. You'll also learn that to feel close isn't so scary, but rather it feels pretty wonderful, and you'll want to experience it again.

Cleaning up the way you communicate will have a positive impact on you and on your marriage.

COMMUNICATION HOMEWORK

Your homework for the coming week is to listen intensely to the way you communicate, and to see if you can clean up one error in communication that you're now aware of making. Also, I'd like you to take the quiz that follows and see if you can (1) spot the errors that the various couples made and (2) state what they should have done differently. Let me warn you, the quiz is a toughie.

The What's-Really-Going-On Quiz

1. Gigi: When you found out you were going to be late, why didn't you call?

   Mike: I didn't think about it. And besides, by the time I stopped and called, I would have been even later.

   Both Gigi and Mike are making communication errors. What should each of them do differently?

   _____

   _____

ANSWER: Instead of asking a question, Gigi needs to make a statement such as, "Mike, you should have telephoned when you found out you were going to be late." Mike, on the other hand, needs to take responsibility for his lateness and apologize.

2. Lois: I'm so aggravated at you for telling that story about me last night.

Ralph: So what's new?

What is Ralph doing in this situation? _____

_____

ANSWER: Ralph is downplaying what Lois has said and acting as though her feelings were unimportant. Also, by suggesting that she always feels aggravated, Ralph is not taking any responsibility for how his behavior contributed to Lois's bad feelings.

3. Alice: I've looked over the finances, and there's no way we can afford a vacation.

Luke: Everyone takes vacations.

What's happening here? _____

_____

ANSWER: Luke is redefining or switching the issue. He shifts from the finances, which Alice is talking about, to the subject of what other people do about vacations.

4. Rose: You've *never heard* of Barbara Mandrell?

What is the hidden agenda? _____

ANSWER: The hidden agenda is: "You're stupid. You don't even know who Barbara Mandrell is."

5. Paul: I'm so busy I'll never get everything done.

Barb: Tomorrow's another day.

What error is Barb making? _____

What might she say instead? _____

ANSWER: Barb is giving Paul a pat answer. She might have said, "What do you have to do?"

6. Lisa and Ron are getting ready to go to a party, and Lisa says, "You're wearing that shirt to the party?"

What should Lisa say instead? _____

ANSWER: Lisa needs to make a statement such as, "Ron, I think you should wear a different shirt," and not ask a question with a hidden agenda.

7. Mark: I just can't seem to get it together in my accounting course.

Rosalie: Why don't you drop the course?

Rosalie is making two errors in communication. What are they?

_____

ANSWER: Rosalie is asking a question with a hidden agenda. The hidden agenda is: "You should drop the course." Also, she is problem-solving too quickly. Instead Rosalie might say, "What seems to be the problem?"

8. Sue: Do you have time to pick up the pork sausage, or do you want me to pick it up?

Barry: Do you plan to grill it outside?

What error is Barry making? What should he say? _____

_____

ANSWER: Barry redefines or switches the issue from picking up the pork sausage to grilling it outside. Barry should respond to Sue's question with either, "Yes, I'll be able to pick it up," or, "No, I don't have the time."

9. Marge: I thought the party was boring last night, didn't you? And I didn't like Bob's comment about women who work and have small children. He always seems to work some put-down about women into the conversation. Don't you agree? And another thing . . .

What's going on here? _____

ANSWER: Marge is acting like Tar Baby by talking on and on. Even when she asks a question, she doesn't give her husband a chance to respond.

10. Judy: When do you think you're going to get the back steps finished, Jim?

    Jim: I've been working on them for the past four weeks.

What's happening here? _____

ANSWER: Jim is redefining or switching the issue. The issue is *when* the steps will be finished, not how long Jim has worked on them. Jim needed to say when he thinks he will finish the steps.

Scoring

There are fourteen possible right answers. If you answered at least twelve correctly, give yourself a pat on the back and an A plus. If you scored less, give yourself a pat on the back for putting in the energy and taking this quiz. And at some point take the time to reread the chapter, for if you want to live Happily Ever After, you'll need to have good communication skills.

MORE GAMES

GAMES COUPLES PLAY

Usually by the third or fourth marriage counseling session I'll ask, "Well, how's it going?" If the person says things are getting better, I'll ask what's making it better. If he tells me he's not sure, I'll push him a little harder. I might ask if *he* has done anything *differently* in the last two or three weeks. Often I'll get a smile and a statement like, "Well, I've been coming home on time. . . . I sent her a funny card one day. . . . I've kept my list." Interestingly, many times people don't want to examine what's making the difference in their marriage, because if they admit openly that what they are doing is making a difference, then they must also take some responsibility when things aren't going so well.

If the response to my question "Well, how's it going?" is "Not so good," I'll press to find out why it's not so good. Is the person doing what he agreed to do? Is he keeping his Do Differently List? With this question I'll often get, "Well, I was keeping my list. But then we had a fight and she got mean. So I decided, the heck with her, and I stopped."

This fellow has just confessed that he's playing the psychological game If-It-Weren't-for-Her.[1] If it weren't for the fact that she got mean, he would be keeping his list. It's all *her* fault that things aren't going well in the marriage.

Each time someone plays a psychological game in a session or tells me about something that occurred during the week that sounds like a game, I'll stop what's going on and take the time to explain the dynamics of that particular game. I do this because I think it's helpful for people to know about games. Unless a person knows about a game, he can't stop playing it. And people need to stop playing games as much as possible because all games end in bad feelings and cause a lot of unnecessary hurt in a relationship.

I still remember the day I was introduced to the concept of psychological games. I had just started my clinical training with a fellow named Morry Haimowitz. He was describing the game ID-I-WIGD-GAR, the acronym for I'll-Do-It-When-I-Get-Damn-Good-and-Ready.[2] His example went something like this.

A fellow had decided that his family needed a new bathroom. So one Saturday, bright and early, he gathered up his tools and carried them to the bathroom. He shut off the water, chipped out some of the ceramic tile, and pulled up the toilet. He then left and went off to the ball game. His wife and kids went to the basement to use an old toilet down there.

The next day this fellow got up, ate breakfast, read the newspaper, cut the grass, and then plopped down in front of the television. About this time his wife said, "When are you going to finish the bathroom?" Two months later the wife and kids were still using the toilet in the basement and the wife was still asking, "When are you going to finish the bathroom?"

When I heard this story, I couldn't wait to get home and tell my husband that the two of us were playing ID-I-WIGD-GAR. For weeks I had been bugging him to caulk around the bathtub. For weeks he had been saying, "Okay," and never quite getting to it. As the weeks passed, I had become more persistent. After all, every time I took a bath, I was reminded about that darned caulking. At night I'd say to him such things as, "Suppose you do the caulking Saturday while I take the boys to their soccer game," or, "How about doing the caulking before our bridge club comes Saturday night?"

Whatever I said, however, didn't seem to get the job done. As the weeks wore on, I clearly was building my case. I now was starting to say to myself, "I can't depend on anybody."

Little did I realize that my husband was also building a case. He was saying something like, "Boy, is she a crab! No matter how much I do, she always has another project for me."

This game was supposed to end with me coming to the end of

my rope and screaming at the top of my lungs, "When are you going to get that *damned* caulking done?" This in turn would invite my husband to yell back, "I'll do it when I get *damn* good and ready!" Fortunately, both of us were saved from reaching this grand finale because I had heard about this game.

When I got home from the workshop that afternoon, I told Skeets about ID-I-WIGD-GAR; I still remember him sitting there with this funny little grin when I told him about the game. And guess what? The next morning when I got up, the caulking was done.

Of course not all games end so abruptly. But once you have the information about a particular game and how it gets played out, it's much easier to stop playing it.

The whole idea of playing games was identified first by Eric Berne, who you may recall wrote the best-seller *Games People Play*. Since Berne's book, others in the helping professions have identified more games that people subconsciously play. And today there is an even better understanding of how these games work and why they are played so often in relationships, even though they ultimately cause bad feelings for everyone involved.

In chapter 2 you discovered your Secret Game Plan. In this chapter I've included other games that couples frequently play. I've given information on why you play a certain game, what you get from playing it, and what specifically you can do to stop playing the game. The first game presented is the ever-popular ID-I-WIGD-GAR.

"I'll-Do-It-When-I-Get-Damn-Good-and-Ready"

In this game one partner makes a request of the other, such as, "Would you please move those ladders along the side of the house?" or, "Would you please get that old trunk we bought out of the hall?" This request is followed by, "Sure, I'll get those ladders put away next weekend," or, "No problem, I'll get that trunk out of there tomorrow." Unfortunately, you know what happens; the ladders stay next to the house, and the trunk remains in the hall.

Finally, the spouse who has made the request yells, "When are you going to get those damn ladders moved?" to which the other spouse yells back, "I'll do it when I get damn good and ready." It may take a few weeks or even a number of months to reach this bottom line. Usually, the longer it takes to play the game to its final conclusion, the more angry each person becomes.

I've seen couples play ID-I-WIGD-GAR about anything and everything. Favorite subjects for this game include discussions about quitting smoking, going on a diet, starting an exercise program, cutting down on drinking, cleaning off one's desk, cleaning the basement, fixing the fence, towing away an old car, and reconciling the checkbook.

The spouse who promises to do something but doesn't do it plays this game to prove that nobody is going to tell him *when* to do something. In addition, he plays to prove that his mate is a bitch and is always on his back about something. The longer the game goes on, the more he can validate his position. And the longer it goes on, the more she can bitch at him. The spouse who doesn't keep his promise also plays because he is afraid of being left, either emotionally, physically, or both. As long as he can keep his mate engaged and in a struggle about something, she'll stay involved in the marriage. Also, the ID-I-WIGD-GAR player does not deal with his anger directly. Instead he procrastinates, which is an indirect way of dealing with his anger.

The partner who keeps asking, "When are you going to do such and such?" plays the game to prove that her spouse cannot be counted on. She is proving to herself that, "If I want something done, I better do it myself." At the end of the game this partner gets to have a "free" temper tantrum; that is, a temper tantrum she feels justified in having. Her tantrum may take the form of a spending spree, a night out with the girls, or a few days of doing what *she* damned well pleases.

How to Stop Playing:

If your spouse verbally agrees to do something but then doesn't actually do it, point out that the job has not been done and together come to an agreement about when it will be done. If it does not get done by the time agreed on, assume that your mate is not going to do it. Then come up with another plan, such as doing it yourself, hiring someone to do it, or deciding that the project simply will have to go undone. Also remember:

1. Don't get into the game again when he says, "Just let me get the garage door painted, and then I'll move those ladders," or you'll find yourself playing round two of ID-I-WIGD-GAR before you know it.

2. Don't say anything more to your spouse about the project,

which will be difficult because your tendency will be to give him one more chance, or one more nudge, and thus continue the game.

I had one woman tell me that if she stopped playing this game, nothing around her house would get done, or worse, she would wind up having to do everything herself because they couldn't afford to have it done. What she was forgetting, however, was that her nudging and pushing did not get the job done but instead only served to build her anger.

This woman would be well advised to do those chores that are essential, such as cutting the grass, feeding the dog, and watering the plants. Those jobs that are not essential, such as cleaning out the garage, could be left to her husband. After all, a garage can go for years without getting cleaned out.

If you're the partner who usually says, "I'll do it," and then you don't, you can break up this game by following through and doing what you agreed to do. Or you can say up front, "I'm not willing to do it," or, "Let's hire someone else to do it. That project is just not a priority with me." All you need to do is take responsibility for your position and state it frankly. You'll save you and your spouse a lot of bad feelings.

"Why-Don't-You/Yes-But"

Another favorite of couples is the game Why-Don't-You/Yes-But.[3] In this game Mike is the Why-Don't-You player and Marsha is the Yes-But player.

Mike: Let's call the Millers and ask them over for dinner.

Marsha: All right, but the house looks like a mess.

Mike: Well, I'll help clean it. It can't take that long.

Marsha: Yeah, but I don't want to spend my whole day cleaning. Besides, I planned to go shopping today.

Mike: So we'll hurry.

Marsha: All right, but that means a trip to the grocery store that I hadn't planned on, and I don't even know what to fix for dinner.

Mike: I'll pick up some steaks. They're easy.

Marsha: Steaks are so expensive. Besides, I don't even think
           Sandy eats red meat.

Mike: So we'll barbecue chicken.

Marsha: Yes, but you know how I hate to cut up chicken.

Mike: Let's just skip it then.

Marsha: Well, that's fine, but we really do need to do some
           entertaining, and the Millers have had us over a lot.

On the surface it appears that Marsha really wants to have company. All she wants are some suggestions about getting the house clean and what to serve for dinner. It also looks as though all Mike really wants is to be helpful and give Marsha suggestions. However, a whole lot more is going on here.

Marsha only wants suggestions so that she can reject them, one by one. Outwardly she's saying, "Help me, Husband," but inside she's saying, "Nobody's gonna tell *me* what to do."

On the other hand, Mike outwardly is operating from the position of Mr. Helpful. Note that all his suggestions are geared to telling Marsha how they can work it out. To himself, however, Mike is confirming what he believes about Marsha and people in general: "People are stupid and ungrateful, and no matter how you try to help them, they never make use of suggestions."

Why-Don't-You/Yes-But is played most often by couples who are in a power struggle over who is going to make the decisions in the relationship. Some days the husband plays helpful ("Let me make a suggestion") and the wife plays helpless ("I can't figure things out"). Other days they switch roles and the wife plays helpful and the husband plays helpless. What's interesting is that with this game both husband and wife are usually adept in either position.

This game is also a favorite of people who "play at" communicating because they are afraid to talk about the more important and more difficult issues in their lives. Perhaps the issues that Mike and Marsha should be talking about are how much money Marsha should spend when she goes shopping, who determines what friends are to be invited over, and who is responsible for doing certain chores. Instead of talking about these issues, however, Mike and Marsha play "verbal Ping-Pong."*

The problem with Why-Don't-You/Yes-But is that when it ends, both players feel frustrated because nothing positive has been accomplished and a lot of time and energy have been expended. The spouse who takes the helpful role and offers one suggestion after another winds up feeling irritated that none of his suggestions is acceptable. And the spouse who takes the helpless role feels discouraged because her mate hasn't been able to come up with a satisfying solution, even though subconsciously she doesn't want a solution.

How to Stop Playing:

If you find yourself taking the position Why-Don't-You in your relationship, here's a good way to get out of this game: Decide that you'll give a maximum of three suggestions, regardless of your partner's response. Then you can extricate yourself from the game by saying, "I'm out of suggestions," or, "You go ahead and decide." This strategy puts the responsibility on your mate and prevents you from giving numerous suggestions and then feeling badly because they're not accepted. It also keeps you from moving to the bottom line and thinking, "People are ungrateful and stupid."

If you find yourself taking the position Yes-But, you can stop the game by saying, "Let me think about it." Then make a decision. You also might say, "Sounds like a good suggestion; let me try it," or, "I've tried that before, but I think it's worth another try."

If you and your spouse are avid Why-Don't-You/Yes-But players, this is going to be a hard game to give up. The reward for both of you, however, is a chance to have a conversation that ends with good feelings.

Come-Here/Go-Away

Another game that husbands and wives frequently play is Come-Here/Go-Away.[4] In this game your spouse invites you to feel warm and close to him. As you start to do so, however, your spouse pulls a switch and—zap—you feel pushed away.

A spouse may play this game by volunteering to do something for his partner (Come-Here) and then not doing it (Go-Away). Or he may ask his mate to do something for him (Come-Here), and then after she has put the plan in motion or has done it, he decides he doesn't want it anymore (Go-Away).

Come-Here/Go-Away is a hard game to spot initially because

there are no buzz words, such as, "When are you going to do such and such?" or, "Why don't you?" and, "Yes, but." The intensity of the feelings that you experience at the end of this game, however, often helps you learn to identify it. And as time goes on, you'll start seeing the pattern that this particular game takes in your marriage.

Here is a typical Come-Here/Go-Away situation:

Monday night

Jean: Darn. The blouse I planned to wear to the meeting Wednesday is at the cleaners.

Sam: Don't worry, honey. I'll pick it up on my way home tomorrow night.

Jean: Oh, good. Thanks a lot.

Tuesday night

Jean: Hi, honey. Did you get my blouse?

Sam: Traffic was so bad coming home I decided to skip the cleaners.

Sam has just pulled a switch on his wife. First he invited Jean to feel she could depend on him by telling her he would pick up her blouse; most of us feel close to someone who volunteers to do something for us. Then he pushed Jean away just as rapidly when he told her he decided to skip the cleaners.

Here's another example of Come-Here/Go-Away:

Morning

Dave: I've been having the worst time of it at work lately. Do you think you could meet me for lunch today?

Ruth: I'll have to rearrange my schedule, but all right. I'll call you right before I'm ready to leave my office.

Noon

Ruth: Hello, Dave. Listen, I'll be ready to leave in about ten minutes. Meet you at the Salad Bowl.

Dave: Uh . . . listen, Ruth, things are really starting to happen around here. I think I'm going to pass on lunch today.

Dave asked Ruth to do something for him (Come-Here). But when she put the plan in motion and changed her schedule in order to meet him for lunch, Dave canceled (Go-Away).

Another example is Karen, who says to her husband, "How about going shopping with me?" Her husband, Vern, says, "Well . . . ummm . . . oh . . . ," stalling as he rearranges in his mind what he had planned to do that day. When he says good-naturedly, "Sure, I'll go. It'll be fun," she says, "Oh, never mind." At this point Vern feels as though the rug has been pulled out from under him.

In the preceding three examples, Jean (the woman who didn't get her blouse), Ruth (the woman who rearranged her schedule), and Vern (the husband who was willing to go shopping) were all innocent players in these games. However, in the next example both the husband and the wife are in collusion as they play Come-Here/Go-Away.

Each year, by November, the husband would start talking about taking a family vacation the following summer. The wife would respond by getting all excited and would start making plans. As April or early May approached, the husband would sit his wife down and tell her that they just couldn't afford the vacation they planned. The wife, of course, would act disappointed, betrayed, and outraged. The husband would try to placate her with suggestions of several day-trips they could take over the summer. When she rejected these suggestions, *he* would become outraged. At that point he saw his wife as an unreasonable person because she *knew* they couldn't afford a vacation.

The wife's seeming unreasonableness allowed him to focus on her behavior. And it allowed him to avoid dealing with his own feelings of inadequacy because he didn't make enough money for the vacation. The wife's anger allowed her to justify emotionally withdrawing from her husband. Both the husband and the wife participated in this yearly game by not deciding in November how much money they could spend on their vacation and where they were going to get the vacation money.

Remember the couple who fought over orange juice? They, too, were in collusion with each other to play this game, because both the husband and wife subconsciously *knew* that she wasn't going to get the orange juice, even though she said she would. Every couple months, however, they played the orange-juice, or Come-Here/Go-Away, game.

Externally, a Come-Here/Go-Away player presents himself as a nice person who wants to please his spouse; internally, he operates from a center-of-the-world position ("I count more than you count"). He feels justified in changing plans without taking his spouse's wants and feelings into consideration. This game also allows him to avoid closeness, something he claims he wants, but something he is afraid of experiencing because it means taking risks and exposing his own inadequacies.

The spouse who cooperates in playing Come-Here/Go-Away also is afraid of closeness and, often, sexual intimacy. What this game confirms for her is that no one will ever take care of her. As a result, she feels alternately angry and depressed, which allows for an additional set of unhealthy payoffs, such as overspending, not getting out of bed in the morning, or doing what she darn well pleases.

How to Stop Playing:

If you realize you've been playing Come-Here/Go-Away, here are a few suggestions for how to avoid this game in the future:

1. Stop making promises to do something unless you are going to do it. And once you make a promise, don't go back on your word, no matter how difficult it is for you.

2. If circumstances should arise that absolutely prevent you from keeping your word, take responsibility and tell your spouse that you are not going to do what you had promised. Apologize *and* do something to make up for it, such as asking her out to lunch. Such an effort will go a long way in taking some of the sting and disappointment out of the situation.

3. Don't ask your spouse for help and then reject the help when it comes.

If the Come-Here/Go-Away game does get played out, however, talk with your spouse about the situation. In the first example, Jean might have said to Sam, "When you volunteered to pick up my blouse from the cleaners, I felt I could trust you. But when I found out that you hadn't picked up my blouse, I felt angry and disappointed. It would have been better if you hadn't said you'd do it in the first place." This confrontation won't get Jean the blouse she wanted for the meeting, but it will make Sam more aware of his behavior. And maybe he won't play this game in the future.

Schlemiel/Schlemazl

Another game couples play far too often is Schlemiel/Schlemazl,[5] (from the Yiddish words meaning "a bungling ne'er-do-well/an unlucky guy"). In this game one spouse will ask the other to do something and the mate will agree. However, when the mate does what he has agreed to do, he messes up in some way: He puts a new light bulb in and gets the shade dirty; she paints the bathroom and gets paint all over the window; he goes to the grocery store and "forgets" items; or she dries the dishes and breaks a few of them. In other words, this spouse plays the Schlemiel (the ne'er-do-well), while his spouse is put in the position of the Schlemazl (the unlucky one). A small variation of this is the mate who actually *volunteers* to do something and then proceeds to mess it up in some way.

Here's an example of the game:

Morning
Elliot: How about picking up some tickets for the Dallas game on your lunch hour, Jan?

Jan: Sure. I'll do it today.

That night
Elliot: Have any trouble getting tickets for the Dallas game? I heard they were nearly sold out.

Jan: Oh, I got tickets for the *Washington* game.

In this situation, Jan is the Schlemiel (she messes up) and Elliot is the Schlemazl (he gets messed over).

Here's another example of the same game with different players:

Before the party
Julie: While I finish getting dressed, will you run to the store and get another bottle of white wine, a couple of bags of ice, and some cocktail napkins?

Burt: Sure.

A half hour later

Julie: You got red wine instead of white, dinner napkins instead
         of cocktail napkins, and you forgot the ice. I can't believe
         it!!

In this instance, Burt is the Schlemiel player, and Julie is the
Schlemazl; Burt is messing up and Julie is being messed over.

Now, if Schlemazl gets angry and confronts Schlemiel on messing
up, Schlemiel acts indignant and suggests that his spouse is being
unreasonable. After all, he didn't *want* to mess up. If, on the other
hand, Schlemazl holds back her anger and says nothing, she is being
made the fool because Schlemiel gets to mess up but doesn't have to
take responsibility for his behavior. An added advantage for the Schlemiel player is that he often gets out of work; his spouse is afraid to
ask him to do anything because he might mess it up.

How to Stop Playing:

If your spouse messes up time after time in your marriage, be
determined that you will keep asking him to do things for you. Also
accept his offers of help. Whatever you do, don't move to the position
"Who needs him" or "I'm better off doing it myself." In the end this
attitude will only get you a lot more work and keep you in a position
of feeling angry with your mate.

Also, your spouse needs to be made responsible for his mess-
ups. For instance, you might say, "Last week when you painted, you
got paint all over the window. So how about cleaning it up?" Or, "I'd
really like you to go back to the store and get the items I asked for."

If you're the spouse who continually messes up, take the time to
think through *why* you mess up. Are you out to prove that your spouse
is an unreasonable person or perhaps a fool? Do you like to see your
spouse angry with you? Do you ever take responsibility for your mistakes? Maybe as a child no one expected this of you. Answering these
questions may help you think through what you get from messing up.
Once you discover the hidden payoffs you receive from this game,
you'll be in a better position to give up this destructive behavior.

Sweetheart

Sweetheart[6] is another game couples play. Here's how it works:

Joyce: How did the meeting go today, Ken?

Ken: Terrible! The boss was in a rotten mood and acted like
         nobody was doing his job. One of the managers got so
         upset that he walked out.

Joyce: By the way, did you notice I mowed the lawn today?

Joyce is a Sweetheart player. She asks her husband how he's doing, not because she wants to know, but because she's a good girl and wants to appear interested. She's a Sweetheart. As her husband tells her how he's doing, she closes him off and says to herself, "How'm I doin', Mom and Dad? Am I acting interested in other people like you taught me?" The answer of course is, "You're doing just fine, Sweetheart." Because Joyce talks to herself instead of listening to her husband, she fails to hear what he's saying.

Spouses who play Sweetheart were usually told as children to be nice and be good to others. They also were expected to "be perfect." When they did what was expected, they were patted on the head and told what a good girl or good boy they were. Soon they learned to live their life for these pats on the head. Rarely did they get pats just because they were somebody's little girl or boy. To get a pat, they had to do something or say something "nice." As adults they ask others, "How did your day go?", "How are you doing?", or, "What's up?" in order to act interested and be nice. But as soon as they ask these questions, they focus inward and hear Mom and Dad say, "You're doing just fine, Sweetheart."

How to Stop Playing:

If you play Sweetheart (and you know if you do), start taking better care of yourself. Start complimenting yourself; start giving yourself more free time; start loving yourself—for it's you who needs the extra care. And ask how your mate is doing only when you really want to know.

If your spouse plays Sweetheart, you might say, "You're not listening," or, "I feel hurt when you ask me about my day and then don't listen to what I say." These confrontations address your spouse's behavior and more than likely will persuade her to start listening to you instead of to Mom and Dad, who live in her head.

Corner

Another destructive game that couples play is Corner.[7] That is, no matter what one spouse does, the other is not satisfied.

One woman complained for months that her husband didn't make enough money. When her husband finally did get a different job and was making more money, however, she switched to complaining about his spending too much time thinking about his darn job.

Another fellow was forever on his wife to try something new when they made love. The morning after she had tried a new approach, however, he accused her of being involved with someone else.

In another Corner game a guy simply won't make a decision about what restaurant to go to, what movie to see, or what he wants for dinner. So his wife makes the decision. And then he's angry because he doesn't like the decision she makes.

There's also the wife who tells her husband to find a hobby and get out and make friends like other husbands. Finally, after months of badgering, her husband joins a bowling team. Is this wife happy? No. Now she pouts because he leaves her on Thursday nights to go bowling.

And consider the wife who tells her husband that he never expresses his feelings. Then, after one very emotional fight, her husband puts his hands over his face and cries. She responds with silence and acts aloof because she doesn't approve of men who cry.

The spouse who plays Corner usually is afraid of intimacy, but instead of being in touch with this fear, she tells her mate that if only he would do this or that, they would be closer. But when her mate responds and does "this or that," the Corner player again finds something to be dissatisfied with and thus continues to avoid closeness.

How to Stop Playing:

Rarely does the partner who has put his mate in a corner perceive himself as doing it. He simply is not aware that his mate is caught between the devil and the deep blue sea. But if the mate who is in the corner can identify the damned-if-I-do corner and the damned-if-

I-don't corner, and explain it, the game is usually over (since most people do not consciously decide to put their mate in a corner).

"If-It-Weren't-for-You"

If-It-Weren't-for-You is another game that husbands and wives frequently play. In this game a spouse will put the blame on his partner for something that is really his responsibility. For example, a husband will tell his friends that he can't possibly go out drinking with them "because of the old lady." In reality, this husband is afraid of people and feels shy and awkward around them. He uses his wife as an excuse to avoid the situation.

Or a woman will tell her friends, "If it weren't for him, I'd have a job, but he doesn't want me to work." In truth, she is unsure of herself and her own abilities. Instead of taking responsibiltiy for her own insecurities, however, she uses her husband as an excuse for not having a job.

Here are a few more examples that illustrate the If-It-Weren't-for-You game. Notice how the If-It-Weren't-for-You player shifts the responsibility for his or her behavior onto the spouse.

- If it weren't for all the drinking he did, I wouldn't spend so much time shopping and always be going off the budget.

- If it weren't for her constant bitching, I would come home earlier at night.

- If it weren't for her sarcastic comments, I would talk to her more.

- If it weren't for all those hours he put in at work, I wouldn't have had an affair in the first place.

- If it weren't for him, I'd go back to school and finish my education.

Usually a person who plays If-It-Weren't-for-You uses these exact words. Sometimes, however, the spouse plays a more sophisticated version of this game and says, "It's all your fault," or, "You know you're the one who wanted to do it in the first place." The most refined player is the spouse who says to her husband at the climax of their game, "Well, you're the one who wanted to marry me!"

A person plays If-It-Weren't-for-You to defend his own behavior while simultaneously putting responsibility for that behavior on his spouse. Usually as a child this person was allowed to blame others in the family for his failures and mistakes. As an adult, he blames his mate. Or, he tries to live by the message "be perfect," and he has a great deal of trouble admitting that he has done anything wrong.

How to Stop Playing:

If you find yourself saying or implying, "If-It-Weren't-for-You," don't allow yourself to use this excuse. Be determined to take responsibility for your own behavior. Once people start taking responsibility for their own lives, they usually find that they accomplish more and feel happier.

If your partner plays this game, you can say, "I want you to stop using me as your excuse. If you want to go bowling, do it. If you want to go back to school, go ahead. The decision is yours."

"Now-I've-Got-You, You-S.O.B."

Another destructive game that many couples play is Now-I've-Got-You, You-S.O.B.[8] In this game one spouse takes the role of the defendant, while the other becomes the accuser. They might play out this game in the following fashion.

Mary and John, having had trouble meeting their bills in the past, decide to go on a budget. Soon after they agree on the budget, Mary goes shopping. At first she is careful, but as the day wears on, she finds herself charging one thing after another. In the next few days John notices that Mary has a new dress, new shoes, new earrings, and a new nightgown. To move the game along and to make it more exciting, however, John says nothing to Mary about what he thinks has happened.

Mary, calculating when each department store sends out its bill, rushes home from work and intercepts each bill as it comes in. John also has a good idea when the bills are to arrive, but he says nothing.

Then comes Saturday. John (the accuser) strolls into the kitchen and says to Mary (the defendant), "By the way, I've finished paying all the bills for the month, but for some reason, we haven't received our department store bills. Do you know anything about them?"

Mary, true to form, denies knowing anything. John, no novice to this game, leaves Mary fixing breakfast while he stalks the house. He rummages through Mary's desk drawers and then goes through her dresser drawers. As he rummages, his angry feelings build. Ah-hah . . . just as he suspected, he finds three bills tucked behind the bedroom mirror. Triumphantly John returns to the kitchen and presents Mary with the evidence. Red-faced and shaking with anger, he dramatically throws each bill down on the table. This gesture translates . . . Now-I've-Got-You, You-S.O.B.

The game may end at this point, with Mary confessing to her crime and pleading forgiveness from John. Or it may go on through the weekend, with Mary continuing to deny that she overspent and John hauling out of the basement the last seven years of canceled checks to prove just how much she has spent. If this game does not provide John and Mary with enough drama and negative attention, it may continue beyond the weekend.

Round two of Now-I've-Got-You, You-S.O.B. may involve John going to the bank on Monday, closing the joint checking account, taking all but a few dollars from the savings account, and writing each department store to cancel the charges. Of course, John does all this without Mary's knowledge. Round two ends when Mary goes to the bank and finds she has almost no money or when she tries to use one of her charge cards.

Another game of Now-I've-Got-You, You-S.O.B. was played by a couple I was working with in counseling.

Lisa walked into the bedroom one morning and said to her husband, "Say, Jeff, did you know the light bulb is burned out in the bathroom?" To which Jeff shrugged and said, "Oh?" (Weeks later, during a therapy session, Jeff actually admitted to me that when Lisa first told him about the light bulb, he had thought to himself, "There's no way I'm going to replace that bulb. If she wants me to replace it, she's going to have to take responsibility and ask.")

Two days after the game had begun, Lisa came back to Jeff and said, "I can't even see to put on my makeup in the bathroom with that burned-out light bulb." And Jeff responded, "Umm . . . umm," and reaffirmed to himself that he was not going to replace that darn light bulb until Lisa asked him directly.

Another week passed, and one morning while they were getting ready for work, Jeff noticed that Lisa was straining to see herself in the mirror, making use of the light that was coming from the hall. At that moment Jeff felt sorry for Lisa, and later that day, when she wasn't around, he replaced the light bulb. The saga continued, however, when Jeff again had a change of heart and decided not to tell Lisa that he had replaced the light bulb and Lisa continued to put on her makeup with the light from the hall.

A few days after Jeff had replaced the bulb, Lisa walked into the kitchen, hands on hips, and said indignantly, "Just when are you going to replace that light bulb?" Jeff looked up from his newspaper, leaned back in his chair, and said, "Why, I replaced it a few days ago, didn't you know?" Which translates . . . Now-I've-Got-You, You-S.O.B.

Other games of Now-I've-Got-You include having your husband followed by a private detective to prove to him at a later time that he is seeing someone else, marking the liquor bottles to prove to your wife at some point that she is drinking again, and asking your husband about a certain incident when you already have all the information in order to prove to him in no uncertain terms that he's a liar.

The spouse who plays Now-I've-Got-You has an affinity for this particular game because it gives him the opportunity to focus on his spouse's bad behavior instead of looking at the inappropriate things *he* does in the marriage. The game also allows him to justify having a temper tantrum, with his spouse as the target, which further allows him to avoid closeness and sexual intimacy. As long as he's angry and feels justified in his anger, he doesn't have to talk with his wife, be nice to her, do things around the house, participate in the family, or have sex with her. The Now-I've-Got-You player is more interested in being vindictive than in working things out. The game also confirms the player's belief that other people can't be trusted.

The spouse who takes the position "I'm innocent until proven guilty" also has a problem with trusting people and getting close to them. Her position in life is that people are untrustworthy—herself included—and that people are fools. If her spouse doesn't catch her, she affirms he's a fool. And if he does catch her and overreacts, she also gets to affirm that he's a fool.

How to Stop Playing:

If you're the spouse who plays Now-I've-Got-You, you need to confront your partner on her behavior long before you build your case. John could have said, "Mary, I know you're off the budget because of all the new things you've been wearing. And I'm angry because you broke our agreement." This confrontation would have served at least to get the problem out in the open. If this couple hadn't switched issues but stuck with Mary's going off the budget and how they were going to reconcile their money situation, the problem could have been solved with a minimum of hurt and anger.

In the light-bulb incident, when Lisa said, "Did you know the light bulb is burned out in the bathroom?" Jeff might have said, "Sounds as though you want me to put in a new light bulb." This way Jeff would have directly addressed the hidden agenda in Lisa's question instead of making the angry decision that he wasn't about to put in a bulb until his wife asked him. What's so sad about this situation is that Jeff still could have saved the day by telling Lisa that he had replaced the light bulb when he did it, instead of setting her up to look like a fool. If he had taken this option, he at least would have gotten a thank-you and maybe a hug or two.

If you're the spouse who plays "I'm innocent until proven guilty," as did Mary (who went off the budget and then hid the bills), you can stop the game by acting responsibly in your marriage. And if you do mess up and get confronted about your inappropriate behavior, take responsibility for it then and there instead of denying what you've done. Nothing is more infuriating than to live with a spouse who doesn't own up to her mistakes. In the light-bulb situation, Lisa needed to ask directly for what she wanted from Jeff. What she might have said was, "By the way, the light bulb is out in our bathroom. Would you replace it?" By asking the question, Lisa takes responsibility for what she wants.

WHY GAMES AND WHY THEY CONTINUE

Unfortunately, all of us play games from time to time because all of us need to confirm what we learned in childhood about ourselves and about other people. If a woman believes that men can't be depended upon, based on her childhood experience with her father who was not emotionally supportive, she's likely to get involved with a man who plays Come-Here/Go-Away (he promises to do something and then he doesn't) or Schlemiel/Schlemazl (he keeps messing up in some way). Both these games allow her to feel disappointed and confirm that she can't depend on a man.

If a man decided early in his life that women are always harping about something because his mother and older sisters were overbearing, he's likely to play I'll-Do-It-When-I-Get-Damn-Good-and-Ready. By not doing what he has agreed to do, he sets up a situation for his wife to be on his case.

People also subconsciously play games for the recognition, or "strokes"*9 that are involved. It's not that someone says, "I think I'll sit down and play a few rounds of Why-Don't-You/Yes-But, which will be a good way to get my husband to talk to me." Instead, the wife starts saying, "Yes, but," to every suggestion her husband makes, which inadvertently serves to invite him to stick around, make yet another suggestion, and talk to her.

Games also help us structure our time together. After all, couples have to have something to talk about. If we're afraid to express our inner thoughts and dreams for fear we will be criticized or laughed at by our mate, we can talk about when the ladders are going to get moved and play I'll-Do-It-When-I-Get-Damn-Good-and-Ready.

I've done a lot of therapy over the years, and I've found that most people aren't bad or mean or out to hurt their spouse. And yet they do. What happens in most instances is that the person is taking care of himself and inadvertently causes his spouse pain. He usually doesn't say, "Ah-ha . . . I'll fix her and not pick up her blouse from the cleaners. I'll play Come-Here/Go-Away." Instead he says, "This traffic is terrible. I'm tired. I'm going home." Of course, the result is that his behavior has an impact on his wife. Because he has made a promise to go to the cleaners and then doesn't, his wife feels hurt and angry and thinks, "After all I've done for him."

Because of these reasons—taking care of yourself, the desire for strokes (whether positive or negative), time structure, and confirmation of what you learned in childhood—you will be tempted to continue to play games. The important thing is that you work at not playing them.

HOMEWORK

Over the next few weeks, try to identify the game or games that you and your spouse are most likely to play. Undoubtedly you'll find one or two. Think about why these are your favorite games and what playing them confirms for you. Then decide what behavioral changes you'll need to make to stop playing the games. In addition, you may want to go back to the sections discussing the games you've caught yourself playing and reread "How to Stop Playing."

A word of caution: After reading this information you may find yourself tempted to tell your spouse, "You're playing a game," acting as if it's all his fault. If you do this, you are now playing Blemish.[10] In this game the goal is to find the fault or flaw in your spouse and then point it out so you can feel better about yourself. When you tell your spouse about a game, say instead, "Let me tell you about the game *we're* playing." This way he won't feel that he is being attacked or that the game is totally his responsibility. Make it *your goal* to stop playing games.

GIVE
YOURSELF
A BREAK

You've probably discovered by now that not all things that go wrong in your relationship are your mate's fault and that you, too, need to change. You have learned, perhaps to your amazement, that you set your mate up by asking questions with hidden agendas, and you often problem-solve too quickly instead of giving your mate a chance to talk about the problem. To your utter surprise, you find that you sometimes play Sweetheart (when your mate is talking to you, you're off in your head making a list of what you need to do tomorrow). Before you started reading this book, you prided yourself on being a good listener and a nice person. And now you're not quite so sure.

Let me reassure you. Setting your mate up or playing Sweetheart sometimes does not cancel out all the other times you do listen and all the good things about you. It simply means that, now that you have discovered you do these things, it's time to change them. I rarely get angry with people when they make a mistake unless their behavior is a deliberate attempt to get even or hurt their spouse. Most people don't mess up deliberately or want to hurt their spouse. They do things to take care of themselves, and inadvertently, as a result of this behavior their spouse gets hurt.

If we were working together in my office, I would be giving you a lot of support. I would tell you not to beat yourself for your mistakes. I would nod, and smile, and compliment you on your willingness to look at yourself. After all, it's not an easy job to look at your behavior. And sometimes you would tell me about something ridiculous you had done, and sometimes I would tell you about something ridiculous I had done. We would have a chance to laugh together, and you would feel better. Each time you looked at yourself and recognized something you didn't like, I would tell you it was good that you were figuring out what you did, because it is the first step to changing your relationship.

So tell yourself you're doing good. Take a minute to give yourself a pat on the back for having the courage to think about your behavior.

The special people of the world are those who are willing to look at themselves and admit that indeed they mess up sometimes. These are the people I can feel closest to because they are willing to share their weaknesses and vulnerabilities. And you are one of those people because you've been willing to read this book and make your marriage better. That makes you special. So don't discount all the terrific and wonderful things about you. Or . . . I'll throw a Nerf ball at you!

6

CHILDHOOD

FOCUSING ON YOUR CHILDHOOD

It's now time to look at your childhood. How did your parents get along? How was anger handled in your family? Who made the majority of the decisions? What kind of relationship did you have with your grandparents? What was your favorite radio or television program? What did the teachers think about you at school? As you explore your childhood, you will be better able to understand yourself and why you often behave as you do in your own marriage.

Remember back to when you were a child and your folks would have an argument and you would think, "I'm never going to act like my parents when I get married. You'll never see me yelling at the top of my lungs like my mother." Or, "I'm never going to walk around pouting like my father." Now that you're married, however, you find yourself saying, "I can't believe it; I sound like my mother." Or, "This is weird, I'm acting just like my father."

You sound and often act like your parents because that's how you learned to act. Even though you may not have liked the way your parents behaved, that's the behavior you were taught. This is the behavior that comes most naturally to you.

You cannot choose what behaviors you were taught. If your family did a lot of yelling and fighting, chances are you're going to be a yeller and a fighter, unless you consciously make a decision not to yell and fight. If your family did a lot of touching and hugging, you're going to be a toucher and a hugger. And if your family did a lot of yelling and fighting and touching and hugging, you're going to be a yeller and a fighter and a toucher and a hugger.

Think back for a minute about your family as you grew up. You may not look like your siblings, but all of you have certain identical mannerisms that were learned over the years from your parents. And if you look at your parents, you'll find they share these same mannerisms with *their* parents. You might say these mannerisms are your family's trademark.

In my family, all the women stand with the backs of their hands resting on their hips, when they're talking. My mother does it. My sister and niece do it. I do it, and my daughter does it. And our grandmother used to do it.

The first time I noticed this peculiar position was when I saw a video of myself giving a talk. I was both astonished and horrified. It's not what one might call a professional stance. Nevertheless, I still catch myself from time to time standing with the backs of my hands resting on my hips. This position just comes naturally because it's the stance that was modeled for me. More important, even though it may look silly, it feels right. To choose a different position while I'm standing and talking to someone takes a conscious effort on my part.

As I was writing this book, my sister read this part of the manuscript, and she telephoned me to say, "I don't stand with my hands on my hips." I said, "Sure you do. You're just not aware of it." Then a week or two later the two of us were talking in the bathroom while I was curling my hair. Suddenly she caught a glimpse of herself in a full-length mirror, and there she was, standing with the backs of her hands resting on her hips. Needless to say, we both had a good laugh over this.

I'm sure you have had the experience of calling a friend on the telephone and thinking that you were talking to your friend, when actually you were talking to your friend's son or daughter. After the children become a certain age, the men in the family start sounding the same, and the women start sounding the same: their pronunciation is identical; they have the same inflection; they structure their sentences in a similar fashion. Again, everyone sounds the same because the children have learned this behavior by watching and listening and modeling. Although nobody said, "Talk like this," everyone does it because that's the behavior that was presented to them day in, day out.

Messages from Parents

When I see someone for marriage counseling, I try to explain that he didn't have much choice about what behaviors he was taught when he was growing up. No one said to him, "Do you want to take a course in Love 101? Or would you prefer the course in Nastiness 101?" You simply take the course that's offered when you're a child and proceed to live your life according to what you were taught. Transactional analysts call this information that you receive over the years your *script messages**; that is, messages that tell you how to behave and what to expect of yourself and of others. When you put all the messages together, they become your script,[1]* or your life plan.

If, for example, your father acted uncomfortable every time you tried to give him a hug, you would soon have gotten the message that touching was not okay, or that touching men was not okay, or that you shouldn't be affectionate. If you grew up in a family that used sarcasm to get a point across, you would be skilled in the use of sarcasm. If your mother was often angry, you might have picked up the message that life's a drag or that you should walk around with a chip on your shoulder. If you are a woman, you might forever find excuses to be angry in life. If you're a man, you also might display a lot of anger, or you might pick out an angry woman to marry. If, on the other hand, your mother was happy-go-lucky and laughed a lot, you would get the message that life was to be enjoyed, and you would tend to see the good side of things and be an optimist.

Last year I told one of our sons that I thought he was doing too many things, with football, tough courses at school, and volunteer work. His response was, "But, Mom, don't you understand? I like to be busy." A few days later, our daughter, who was six at the time, asked me about taking an art course on Saturday. I told her that I thought she was already involved in enough after-school activities with gymnastics and swimming. She replied, "But, Mom, don't you know I like to be busy?" She also told me this with her hands resting on her hips.

Clearly our children have been scripted to be involved in many things and to "be busy." Neither my husband nor myself has said directly, "Be busy," but we certainly have modeled this behavior for them through the years.

If you grew up in a family that was always on the brink of financial disaster, you may, as an adult, live your life on the brink of financial disaster. You could do this by staying in a job that never quite pays enough money. Or you might make a lot of money and risk losing everything by getting involved in high-risk ventures. You could leave one job before you had another lined up. You could choose a mate who is a compulsive spender. Or you might make lots of money and live like a miser as a way to insure against financial disaster. Whatever variation you choose, you will subconsciously set up your life either to play this theme out or to guard against playing it out. Regardless of what course you take, the message you received in childhood about living your life on the brink of financial disaster has a definite impact on your life today.

One of my favorite stories about how people choose to live their lives was told by Hans Selye, a famous physician and scientist. The story goes as follows:

Two boys were raised by an alcoholic father. When their father was no longer able to care for them, they were placed in different homes. Years later the boys were tracked down and interviewed by a psychologist who was studying alcoholism and its effect on a family. The psychologist found a striking difference in how these men were now living their lives. One had become a helpless alcoholic, whereas the other was a successful, clean-living teetotaler. When the psychologist asked the alcoholic what had been the moving force in his life, the alcoholic replied, "With a father like that, what would you expect?" When the psychologist asked the successful, clean-living teetotaler what had been the moving force in his life, he replied, "With a father like that, what would you expect?"[2]

Clearly you have no more choice about the script messages you receive than you do about who your parents are. You do, however, have a choice as to the way you follow these messages and how much you allow them to affect your life.

You might also receive two conflicting messages, and as impossible as it seems, you will follow both. You may alternate them, choosing to follow first one and then the other, or you may play out both of them simultaneously.

For instance, a man may be very successful in his job, and the night before the announcement that he is to take over as president, he gets drunk, calls the chairman of the board, and tells him off. Or he is very successful in his job and has a miserable personal life.

In addition to receiving script messages through everyday modeling, as a child you are given direct verbal messages about yourself, how to live your life, and what to expect from it.

Parents often tell children that they are pretty, or stupid, or sweet, or no good. Parents also tell children not to feel scared, not to get angry, or to "knock the guy's block off if he gives you trouble." And because children give their parents a lot of power, they usually listen to these messages and often incorporate them into their own thinking. At the same time, *children ultimately determine what messages they will follow and how they will follow them.*

For example, if Marie hears from her mother over and over, "I wish you had never been born," when Marie grows up, she may live her life as a recluse and pretend that she had never been born. She may become a high achiever to prove that Mom was wrong and that someday her mother will be sorry for saying such a thing. Or she may kill herself.

If a child is told over and over, "Why can't you *ever* do anything right?" the child probably isn't going to do much that is right. When he grows up, he will continue to mess up and subconsciously invite other people, including his wife, to say, "Why can't you ever do anything right?" Or he may choose to live out this message by giving up before he gets started. Then his parents and wife might lament, "Why can't you ever do *anything*?" Or the person may flip the message over and become a perfectionist.

If a mother continually tells her daughter, "You're stupid," this message is going to have an impact on the daughter's life. When the daughter grows up, she may fully meet her mother's expectations and do one stupid thing after another. She may also choose to marry a man who thinks women aren't worth much and who also tells her she's stupid. Or she may flip the message over and, instead of acting stupid herself, set out to prove that others, including the man she married, is stupid. Or she might excel academically to prove that she is not stupid.

If a son constantly hears from his father, "You just can't trust anyone nowadays," the son will grow up having an issue around trust. He may subconsciously get involved with people who are untrustworthy. When he gets taken advantage of, he can say, "I knew it, you just can't trust anyone nowadays." Or he himself may be untrustworthy.

One fellow I saw in counseling had the following story. When his father asked him, "What do you want to be when you grow up?" he replied, "I want to be a doctor." To which his father said, "You're too dumb to be a doctor." This response was doubly sad because the man was extremely bright and his father was a doctor. The messages the son received from his father's comment were: "You're stupid," "Don't be a doctor," and, "Don't compete with Dad."

In addition, no one in this family ever said anything to the boy about what he could or would do when he grew up. By the time the man became involved in counseling, he was thirty-two years old, had had a series of get-nowhere jobs, and felt like a failure. He also had married a woman who constantly told him he was a loser. What this man needed was for someone to give him permission to be smart, to compete, and to be successful in life.

Clearly, the messages your parents gave you determine to some extent the course of your life. It's as though they presented you with a how-to book for living. *You decide, however, what messages you will follow and how you will follow these messages.*

Messages from Outside Influences

Parents are not the only ones who give children messages about life and how to live it. Siblings, grandparents, stepparents, aunts, uncles and neighbors also play an important part in a child's scripting.

My Grandma Wild certainly made an impact on my life. While growing up, I would visit her on weekends, and during the summer she would sit for hours with me and play dominoes and checkers. When I was about seven, she gave me an autograph book for my birthday. When I gave her the book to sign, she wrote me the following poem:

My Dearest Doris Ann,

Sing away your life,
Happy may you be,

Loved by all,
But most surely by me.

Anna Wild

Her poem made me feel so loved; I remember walking around on the playground and saying it over and over in my head. It wasn't until years later that I found out that the poem wasn't an original, and that other people used this same poem in autograph books. But in no way did the discovery take away from the importance or the impact the poem had on me. The messages I got from her poem were "Be happy" and "You are very loved."

The media also play an important part in one's scripting, as was clearly illustrated to me one morning about 3:00 a.m. when my daughter came into our bedroom with her cover and her stuffed animal Snoopy. She said she'd had a bad dream and could she please stay with me. Reluctantly, I said sure, but I also said she would have to lie very quietly so I could fall back to sleep. Then she said in the sweetest little voice, "Mom, do you want me to sing you a lullaby? Because on *Sesame Street*, when Burt can't fall asleep, Ernie sings him a lullaby."

I suspect that there is a whole new generation of lullaby singers out there because of Ernie and Burt.

One Traumatic Event

Children also make script decisions based on traumatic events that occur as they are growing up. A parent will die unexpectedly, and a child will make the script decision that he's never going to trust anyone again, or he's never going to let himself get close to anyone for fear something bad will happen. Once he has made these script decisions, he will set his life up in some way to follow them. He may pick out people who are untrustworthy and who in the end will leave him. Or he will be untrustworthy and leave people—either physically, as in a divorce, or emotionally, by keeping others at arm's length.

I've seen a number of women in counseling who had been raped as adolescents. Almost without exception, each of them married men whom they considered either mentally, financially, or socially below them. The reasons given: "I didn't deserve better," or "After what happened, I didn't think I was worthy."

Sometimes an incident may not look like a traumatic event to the outside world, but for the child involved, it has a tremendous impact on the way she lives her life. I think the following story is a good example.

"When I was about seven," said Lori, "my parents asked me to bring down a box of detergent to the basement. When I carried it down the steps, I somehow got it turned upside down and it all spilled out. My father said I had done it on purpose, which I hadn't, and he broke two yardsticks over my legs. I remember running upstairs screaming, and that night I decided that I would never make a mistake again. This decision was impossible to keep, but it made me strive to be perfect and also caused me to beat myself over the head for days when I messed up. And when anyone pointed out a mistake I had made, I was overly defensive. Never did I want to feel such humiliation again."

Recurring Traumatic Events

The children who receive some of the most destructive script messages are those who are abused either sexually or physically on an ongoing basis and those who live in a family where one or both parents are active alcoholics. These children almost always make script decisions that life is scary and people can't be trusted.

The child who is physically or sexually abused comes to expect that others will abuse him and take advantage of him. Consequently, he often sets his life up to be abused and taken advantage of.

One woman I saw in therapy came because her four-year-old daughter had been sexually abused by this woman's father, who also had sexually abused this woman as a child. Within a month of therapy it became apparent that the four-year-old daughter was also being abused by her own father. When she was a child, this woman had received the message "Men abuse you." When she grew up, she married an abusive man, who in turn physically abused her and sexually abused their daughter.

The following diagram illustrates how the message "Be abused" was passed from one generation to another in this family.

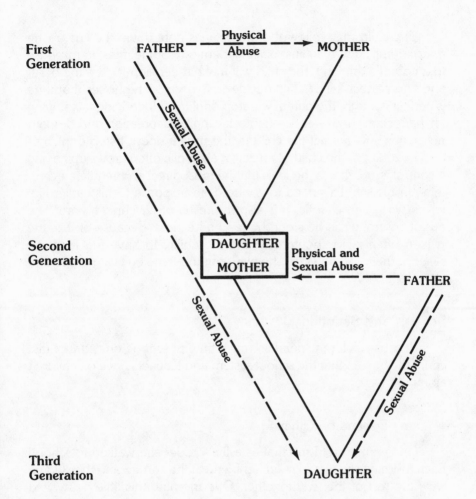

Sometimes the script messages "Don't trust people," "Be taken advantage of," and "Be abused" get turned over, and when the child grows up and gets married, he becomes the spouse who is not trustworthy, who takes advantage, and who is the abuser.

The child of an active alcoholic also experiences one traumatic event after another. This child receives script messages not to think, not to feel, not to be emotionally close to others, not to be responsible or dependable, not to be trustworthy, and to be a drinker.

The child may follow these messages right down the line, or he may carefully guard against playing them out. Sometimes, in response to a parent's drinking, the child will make a decision to "be the best" and "be perfect." The child decides this because he hopes that if he is perfect enough, the parent will stop drinking. Underlying this striving for perfection, however, is often a feeling of depression and despair; no matter how perfect the child is, the parent doesn't stop drinking.

In addition, the child of an active alcoholic often grows up having a control issue; that is, he feels that he must direct and regulate everything in his life. This need to control is in response to his earlier life, which was often chaotic. It is also the result of watching a parent be out of control while he stood by feeling helpless. Because of this, the person often lacks spontaneity and the ability to have fun for fun's sake. Sometimes, however, he plays out this issue by living a wild and crazy life.

Schools and Scripting

Because children spend so much time at school, one cannot discount the impact that the school system and teachers have on children along the way.

● "Don't Depend on Others"

One woman told me that as a first-grader she walked to school. Each morning she would meet her friend at the corner, and they would walk the rest of the way together. One morning this little girl waited and waited, but her friend never came. Finally she went on to school. When she arrived, the teacher said, "You're late," and made her stand in the corner.

When the child tried to explain to the teacher that she had been waiting for her friend, the teacher looked at her and said, "You can't depend on others."

To this day this woman has had trouble trusting people. And if she has something important that needs to be done, she refuses to let others help her, even if it's going to the post office to mail an important letter. She also confessed with a little chuckle that when her car pool is late in the morning, her heart beats faster, she feels sick to her stomach, and she wonders if they have forgotten her.

● "You Indian Giver"

Another woman told the following story. "When I was in grade school I bought my lunch, which was twenty-five cents a day. We had to pay in advance. One day I was sick, so the following week my dad told me to get my quarter from the teacher for the lunch I had missed. When I asked the teacher for it, she took a quarter out of her pocket and threw it on the floor and called me an Indian giver in front of all the other children. I felt embarrassed and humiliated for weeks." Today this woman is overly generous—almost to a fault. The reason: "No one will ever accuse me again of being selfish."

● "Who Would Want You?"

A man said he suffered terribly during gym class and had felt for years that he wasn't good enough. "When we picked teams, I was always the last one chosen. Someone had to take me. No one wanted me." When he first came for counseling, he was afraid of people, overly shy, and worried that others didn't want him around.

● "Say San Francisco"

One woman said that when she was in fourth grade, the teacher walked around the room and asked each child to pronounce or spell a particular word. The word she was given was "San Francisco." When she tried to say "San Francisco," the words wouldn't come out right—not because she wasn't trying, but because she had a speech impediment. The teacher insisted she say the word again and again. After many tries she started to cry, then wet her pants in front of the class. To this day this woman says that when she knows she's going to have trouble with a word, she avoids it at all costs. Also, she is extremely sensitive to others' feelings.

● "Nobody Likes You"

I still remember my third-grade Valentine's Day party. As is the tradition, everyone brought valentines to school for their friends and put them in a large, decorated valentine box that sat on the teacher's desk. On Valentine's Day the cards were given out to the students.

After we received our cards, the teacher asked us to count our valentines. Then she went down the aisle and asked each of us how many we had received. As we gave her the number, she wrote it on the blackboard. The child who got the most valentines was given a prize, as was the child who got the least. The child who received the least was named Marilyn; I had received one more valentine than she had.

I can still see Marilyn's face and her trying desperately to hold back her tears. I felt so badly for her, and for myself. For years I was afraid of going to a party if I didn't know other people there, because I was convinced they wouldn't like me. Thank goodness I had my grandmother's poem to recite.

● "You're Awfully Bright"

Schools also provide children with positive experiences, as one woman attested to. "Up until seventh grade I was an average student. Then I had this teacher who I thought was terrific. One day after I had turned in a history report, she said to me, 'You really are a smart little girl.' That day I walked out of school dancing. Funny thing: after her comment my grades improved dramatically, and I graduated from eighth grade number one in my class. That teacher told me I could excel, and I took her up on it."

I'm sure you, too, can recall at least one incident (good or bad) that occurred during school that made a difference in your life as a child and is still affecting your life. You can now look at that incident with more understanding, and if you need to you can make a redecision about how you will let that incident affect your life today.

FIGURING OUT SCRIPT MESSAGES

To further understand yourself and why you sometimes behave as you do, it's helpful to know what specific messages you received as a child. You can then look at a particular message and see what you are doing to live it out. You can choose to continue to follow the message, or you can decide to modify it in some way. Or you might decide that it causes you too much pain and that you need to stop following the message altogether. The important thing is that discovering your script messages will free you to choose and change.

If your family gave you the message "You're not as smart as your brother," and as a result you have always shied away from anything that seemed too cerebral, you might want to rethink this message and make an effort to start seeing yourself as smart. Once you do this, you'll stop discounting yourself. You may even give yourself permission to go back to school, or to go after a better job, or to start speaking up more to your husband and sharing what you think instead of giving all the power to him.

Messages about Self-Worth

Here are some of the more common messages that children receive about their looks, personality, and talents. Put a check mark by the ones you received while growing up.

- ☐ You're too heavy.
- ☐ You're pretty.
- ☐ You're handsome.
- ☐ You've got a good voice.
- ☐ You're clumsy as an ox.
- ☐ You're a bad boy.
- ☐ You're a brat.
- ☐ You're terrible with figures.
- ☐ You should be an artist.
- ☐ Be a man.
- ☐ You drive me crazy.
- ☐ Kids are nothing but trouble.
- ☐ You're a jerk.
- ☐ Children should be seen and not heard.
- ☐ You're too big for your britches.
- ☐ You're a nuisance.
- ☐ You have bird legs.
- ☐ You have nice hands.
- ☐ You're smart.
- ☐ You'll never be good in sports.
- ☐ You're a good athlete.
- ☐ You're a good girl.
- ☐ You're slow as molasses.

- ☐ You're sweet.
- ☐ You've got a good head on your shoulders.
- ☐ You'd make a good doctor.
- ☐ You're kind.
- ☐ You're nasty.
- ☐ When will you ever grow up?
- ☐ You're a manipulator.
- ☐ You're a smart-mouth.
- ☐ Shut up.
- ☐ You're always messing up.
- ☐ You're dependable.
- ☐ You're just like your father.
- ☐ You're just like your mother.
- ☐ You'll never amount to anything.
- ☐ You've got what it takes.
- ☐ You're a worrywart.
- ☐ You're never going to make it in this world with that attitude.
- ☐ You're too competitive.
- ☐ Your mouth is going to get you into trouble one of these days.

In addition, write down other messages that come to mind about your looks, your personality, and your talents. If you're not accustomed to writing in books because Mom or Dad told you not to write in books, and every time you do you feel guilty, write the messages on a separate piece of paper. Or rethink this message and give yourself permission to write in this book and not feel guilty.

_____

_____

_____

Messages about Feelings

Children receive a great many messages about feelings—what feelings are okay to have, what feelings are okay to express, and what feelings are not okay to have or to express. Here are some of the more common messages about feelings that children receive either directly or indirectly. Again, check off the ones that apply to you.

☐ Don't be scared.
☐ Be scared.
☐ Life's scary.
☐ You're a crybaby.
☐ Big boys don't cry.
☐ Don't be a sissy.
☐ You're always angry about something.
☐ We don't get angry in this family.

☐ Don't say what you feel.
☐ Life's depressing.
☐ You're a pouter.
☐ You have a chip on your shoulder.
☐ Laughter makes the world go around.
☐ Enjoy life.
☐ Keep smiling.
☐ You have a great laugh.

What other messages do you recall receiving about feelings?

_____

_____

_____

Messages about Life in General

Children also receive countless messages about life and what to expect from it. Following are some of the more common messages given to children either directly or indirectly. Notice the number of clichés that are used to influence a child. Some of these clichés were used not only by your parents, but by your grandparents and your great-grandparents. Check off the messages that apply to you.

☐ If you want something done, do it yourself.

☐ If you're down, the only way to go is up.

☐ Life's too damn hard.

☐ Beauty is only skin deep.

☐ Nothing ventured, nothing gained.

☐ Marry rich.

☐ A little hard work never hurt anyone.

☐ Never believe a woman, not even a dead one.

☐ God helps those who help themselves.

☐ Prosperity is just around the corner.

☐ Stick to your guns.

☐ Turn the other cheek.

☐ Men have all the power.

☐ You'll never know until you try.

☐ Two wrongs don't make a right.

☐ Behind every successful man is a woman.

☐ Never say die.

☐ You'll never grow up.

☐ Idle hands are the devil's workshop.

☐ Money is the root of all evil.

☐ It's always darkest before the dawn.

☐ The grass is always greener.

☐ Don't count your chickens before they're hatched.

☐ A bird in the hand is worth two in the bush.

☐ If at first you don't succeed, try, try again.

What other messages can you recall receiving? Make the effort to write them here.

_____

_____

_____

A SCRIPT CHECKLIST FOR UNLOCKING YOUR PAST

Perhaps the best way to get in touch with the messages you received as a child is to answer a series of questions I've designed to tug at your memory. Taking the time to answer these questions will be invaluable in helping you understand why you behave as you do in your marriage. Notice that the first set of questions is already answered to help familiarize you with using this tool. After you read over the questions and answers, you'll be asked to fill out your own Script Checklist.[*3]

Carolyn's Completed Script Checklist

1. **As a child growing up, what kind of a marriage did you think your parents had? Why?**
   "I think they had a pretty good one. They did a lot of things together and seemed to like each other. They would fight but they always made up."

2. **How did your father show his love to your mother?**
   "He would give her a hug, and sometimes he would reach out and give her a pinch on the fanny. Us kids would laugh when that happened."

3. **How did your mother show her love to your father?**
   "She would cook him nice meals, keep the house clean, and give him hugs."

4. **What do you do to show your love to your spouse?**
   "I cook, keep the house clean, give my husband hugs, tell him I love him, and sometimes I pinch his fanny."

5. **What did your father do when he disagreed with your mother?**
   "He wouldn't talk sometimes, or he'd go in the basement and bury himself in his workshop. He was a pouter when things didn't go his way."

6. **What did your mother do when she disagreed with your father?**
   "She'd get upset and scream and then cry."

7. **What do you do when you disagree with your spouse?**
"I used to get upset, scream, and cry. Over the past few years I've learned to handle my anger better."

8. **How was money handled in your parents' marriage, and were there any problems with money?**
"I think my folks handled their money quite well. Dad got paid on Friday nights, and right after dinner he and Mom would go to their bedroom, sit on the bed, and divvy up the money to pay the bills. Occasionally they would bicker about priorities. I think the biggest problem was that there wasn't much money."

9. **Who controls the money in your marriage?**
"We both work and put our money in a joint checking account. When either of us wants something, we write a check. I don't think we have ever fought about money. I also think we both are conservative, and we know how much we can safely spend before there's a problem. My husband pays bills twice a month, but I have a good idea what the bills are."

10. **Who made most of the decisions in your parents' marriage?**
"My mom."

11. **Who makes most of the decisions in your relationship?**
"We both make decisions; my husband in some areas and I in others. On a daily basis, I make the decisions. If I look back over the years, however, when there has been a difference of opinion he has usually gotten his way. I think it's easier for me to give in."

12. **What messages did your parents send you about sex, verbally and nonverbally?**
"Dad never said anything about sex that I remember. But I know he liked it because of pinching my mom. My mom said flat out sex was fun, but you should wait until you were married before you had it. My mom and dad touched a lot, and sometimes on Sundays they'd go into the bedroom and tell us children not to bother them. They were messing around and we knew it. But nobody ever said anything. It was one of those unwritten rules."

13. **How have the messages you received about sex affected you?**
"I have always enjoyed sex, and I think I have a healthy attitude about it."

14. **What did your father and mother think about men and women, and why?**
"My dad was a little afraid of both men and women, probably because his father died when he was a child and he didn't have a man around to relate to. And his mother was pretty stern with him. I think my mom was afraid, too, but she pushed herself to be friendly and outgoing."

15. **Was your family religious? What part does religion play in your life today?**
"My family went to church each week, and I think this made us all try harder to get along and be nicer to each other during the week. We all believed that if we followed the commandments and did as we were supposed to, we would be rewarded; if we didn't behave, we'd be punished. When I misbehaved, my parents would state, 'Honor thy Father and thy Mother.' I guess you might say my folks pulled rank. Over the years, formalized religion has played a less important part in my life. But on the inside I'm very religious."

16. **Was there much sickness in your family, and what did your mother and father do when someone got sick?**
"Rarely did anyone get sick. I cannot remember a day that my dad stayed home from work because of illness. Occasionally one of us girls would get sick, and Mom would make us a special breakfast of tea and toast and serve it to us in bed. Mom was great that way. She'd also sit with me on the side of the bed and scratch my back and talk."

17. **How do you act when your spouse is sick? How does your spouse act when you are sick?**
"I take good care of my husband when he gets sick. But if he is sick more than a few days, I start to feel irritated, like, 'Come on, enough. Get back to work.' When we first got married and he got sick with the flu, I brought him tea and toast and sat on the edge of the bed ready to talk and rub his back. But he wanted to be left alone. This hurt my feelings. When I get sick, my husband tends to leave me alone and I'm always calling him into the bedroom to talk to me. I think I'm better about bringing him tissues, medicine, and things like that, but I think he is really more

understanding and tolerant when I'm sick. He doesn't seem to put the pressure on to hurry up and get back to work."

18. **When you were a child, who did the chores in the family?**
"My dad cut the grass and repaired the car and did all the outside painting. Mom took care of the inside of the house and told us girls what to do."

19. **Who does the chores in your family?**
"I used to take care of the inside of the house and my husband took care of the outside, but now that's changing. I still tend to take more responsibility with the children and tell them what's expected of them."

20. **What did your parents do for fun?**
"They would have friends over on Saturday night and play cards. Or they would go to someone else's house to visit or play cards. Sometimes on Sunday they would have friends over for dinner. My mom's a great cook. In the summer we'd go camping, fishing, and swimming. Every year we'd take a vacation. This was a big thing; my parents would save all year long for their vacation. Also, we laughed a lot. We'd all sit at the dinner table, and my dad would say something and we'd all laugh until tears ran down our faces."

21. **What do you and your spouse do for fun?**
"We have friends over for dinner. We go out for dinner, go to shows and movies, shop, garden, have sex, and occasionally take a trip. And we laugh a lot. And sometimes we sit side by side and read."

22. **Did your parents have a favorite motto or saying, and what was it?**
"They used to say children should be seen and not heard. And sometimes when Mom was aggravated with me and wanted to put me in my place because she didn't like how I was acting, she would say, 'Who do you think you are, Astor's plush horse?' Also, Mom used to say, 'Work before play.' "

23. **How have these sayings or mottoes affected your life?**
"I think the thing about children being seen and not heard reinforced my shyness. And the comment about Astor's plush horse

made me extremely sensitive and afraid of what others might think of me. I think that comment was pretty degrading. It wasn't until a few years back that I could even tell anyone about it. And when I did, I couldn't stop crying. The work before play has also made its impact. I have trouble relaxing and giving myself free time. I can always find work to do. My working is sometimes annoying to my husband and my friends. And now my parents say, 'Relax. Life's too short to work all the time.' "

24. **What did your parents praise you for when you were little?**
"For watching my sister and keeping the house clean and ironing. I was a great ironer. I remember I used to iron Dad's shirts and I'd leave them hanging on the shower curtain rod in the bathroom until Mom got home from work so she could see how much I had done."

25. **What do you praise yourself for?**
"Certainly not for ironing, because I don't iron anymore. But I do a lot of things and I accomplish a great deal. And I tell myself I'm a good person for doing so much."

26. **When things went wrong in your family, what feelings were your mother and father most likely to have—mad, sad, scared? How did you know your parents felt this way?**
"My mom would feel mad and yell when things went wrong. In fact, she used to yell so loud that all of us would race around the house shutting the windows so the neighbors didn't hear. My dad would also get mad, but he was more controlled with his anger. When he got angry you could feel it in the air, and everyone would tiptoe around."

27. **What is the feeling you are most likely to experience when things go wrong? What do you do to express this feeling?**
"I feel mad and yell and sometimes worry that the neighbors can hear me."

28. **Did you have any brothers or sisters? What was your relationship like with them?**
"I have one younger sister. I think our relationship was a good one. In some ways I felt like her mother because I used to baby-sit her a lot. I'd make her waffles for breakfast; I'd watch her swim in a little wading pool in our backyard; I'd fix her lunch. Sometimes

I would pull her hair when she wouldn't do what I told her to do. Then I'd bribe her with a soda so she wouldn't tell on me. Today she tells me she's addicted to soda because of me. We laugh about this a lot. I used to watch her sometimes when we rode in the back seat of the car. It was almost as if I were studying her, and I thought how pretty she was. Also, she always gave me the last half of her ice cream cone. I'd eat mine and then I'd eat the rest of hers. I always thought she was very generous. I loved her a lot. Still do."

29. **Did you have a favorite childhood story, or hero, or radio or television show when you were a child? How do you think this affected your life?**
"I think my favorite story was 'Pinocchio.' I liked two things about that story. One is that my grandmother sat in her rocking chair and read it to me over one summer. And the story fit with my black-and-white notion about life. If you were good and did things 'right,' you'd be rewarded, whereas if you were bad and did things wrong, you'd be punished. I also had this funny idea that if my nose would grow long when I told a lie, I would never lie. I tried to be good as a child, and anything that would help keep me good, including my nose growing longer, would have been appreciated. Today I'm not nearly so judgmental about myself or others."

30. **What did your parents tell you about school and/or education?**
"My parents didn't say much about school, but my dad used to tell me all the time that the way to get ahead was to get a good education. I must have heard that weekly."

31. **How has what they said about school and education affected your life?**
"I went to college and graduate school, and at age twenty-seven I started my own business. I also picked a man who was very smart and educated. That was a big requirement with me when I dated. I wanted someone with brains."

32. **What did your father and mother want you to be when you grew up?**
"My dad used to say I'd make a great senator. I have no idea why he said this because I don't think he was even interested in politics except during the presidential campaigns. He also used

to tell me when I smart-mouthed my mom that I would make a great lawyer. My mom used to tell me that I should be a secretary. And it was also expected that I would get married and have children, although neither of my parents told me directly to get married and have children."

33. **How have these messages affected your life?**
"I have always had a career. I got married. And I have children."

34. **When you were a child, what did you think was wrong with your father (physically, emotionally, socially)?**
"I thought his nose was too big. I probably thought that because my mom used to say, 'You have a big nose, just like your father.' Actually, my father's rather handsome. I also thought he was about the nicest person I knew. He was kind, gentle, honest, and a great storyteller. And he loved to laugh. The only thing I didn't like was that he worked in a factory. I felt embarrassed by this, and I hated myself for feeling this way."

35. **When you were a child, what did you think was wrong with your mother (physically, emotionally, socially)?**
"I thought she got on my dad's case too much. It was like she was always hounding him about something. I see them differently now, and if I had been my mom, I probably would have hounded my dad, too. He was passive when it came to disciplining us kids, which left her with all the disciplining. But as a child, I didn't understand that."

36. **What did you think was wrong with you and why?**
"I thought I was ugly because of my nose, and my mom used to tell me that one of my toes was too big. I remember when I was at the swimming pool, I'd hide my feet with a towel. And when I dated, I tried not to let the boy see my profile. Also, my mom used to say, 'You can't carry a tune in a paper bag.' On this item she was right. I have a lousy voice. But I still sing when I'm by myself. And I used to sing to my children when they were young. They liked my singing."

37. **Is there anything that happened in your childhood that you think was especially significant? What was it?**
"I was very sick, I think with a throat infection. I guess I was about five years old, and Santa Claus came to visit me. I can still re-

member being in bed and seeing Santa Claus. When he left, I kept saying, 'Santa Claus came to *see me*, Santa Claus came to *see me*.' I think I've always felt a little special because of that incident. Another thing, I had to have my tonsils taken out, and my father took an extra job to pay for the operation. Nobody said much about what he did, but secretly I felt that he must have really loved me to do that."

38. **Is there anything that happened in your childhood that you think has affected your marriage significantly today? What was it?**
"I think my mom got too angry when I was a child. And I get too angry sometimes."

39. **If you could have changed anything about your parents' marriage when you were young, what would it have been?**
"That my mom would have been more tolerant and my father would have taken a more active part in parenting. And that my parents would have had a little more money so they wouldn't have worried so much about the bills and worked so hard all the time. Our family really lived from paycheck to paycheck when I was a child. Also, I wish my parents would have told me I was a good kid and praised me more and told me I was pretty."

40. **If you could change anything about your marriage just by wishing, what would it be?**
"That I was more easygoing. And that my husband would compliment me more and give me more hugs and take charge more with the children."

Looking at the answers to these questions, one can see that this woman's script messages include the following:

Fight and make up.
Be affectionate.
Have a temper—escalate.
Cook and clean to show your love.
Men are passive.
Show your feelings.
Be a pouter.
Be careful with money.

Women run the show.
Sex is fun.
Don't have sex until you're married.
Be afraid of people.
Be friendly and outgoing.
Be religious.
Honor thy Father and thy Mother.
Don't be sick.

Take care of people when they're sick.

Women are in charge of the house.

Men are in charge of the outside.

Women take care of the children.

Enjoy life.

Be happy.

Behave yourself.

Work before play.

Yell when things go wrong.

Be responsible for others.

Do good and you'll be rewarded.

Get a good education.

Have a career.

Get married and have children.

Your nose and toes are too big.

You can't sing.

You're special.

Most of these messages have made an impact on Carolyn's life in one way or another. One message she never followed, although frequently modeled by her father, was to be a pouter. "I have to talk about what's going on. I'm not good at holding it in," she says. Messages she has discarded, although at one time they certainly influenced her behavior, are the ones about her nose and toes. She also doesn't believe she is responsible for the inside of the house. At the same time, she feels anxious if things become too messy, and she often takes responsibility and cleans up the mess even though she didn't make it. This indicates that she still allows herself to be heavily influenced by this message. Carolyn works hard not to follow the messages to fight and yell and have a temper. Over the years she has also become quite comfortable with people, and only on occasion does she feel shy and afraid. She has decided to continue to follow the messages to be affectionate, be friendly and outgoing, enjoy life, and be happy. And she thinks sex is fun.

Your Script Checklist

Now it's your turn to fill in a Script Checklist. If you are not able to remember specifically what happened in your childhood, simply write down how you think it was, because your perception of what went on in your family is really more important than what actually happened. If your parents were divorced when you were young, or if one of your parents died when you were a child, fill in your answers by focusing on the person or persons who raised you.

If you're not willing to fill out this questionnaire, at least answer the questions in your head. I think you'll find that it will be well worth every bit of energy you put into it. The information you receive from answering the questions will give you insights about yourself that you would not have believed possible. It may change your life.

1. As a child growing up, what kind of marriage did you think your parents had? Why?

_____

_____

2. How did your father show his love to your mother?

_____

_____

3. How did your mother show her love to your father?

_____

_____

4. What do you do to show your love to your spouse?

_____

_____

5. What did your father do when he disagreed with your mother?

_____

_____

6. What did your mother do when she disagreed with your father?

_____

_____

7. What do you do when you disagree with your spouse?

_____

_____

8. How was money handled in your parents' marriage, and were there any problems with money?

_____

_____

9. Who controls the money in your marriage?

_____

_____

10. Who made most of the decisions in your parents' marriage?

_____

_____

11. Who makes most of the decisions in your relationship?

_____

_____

12. What messages did your parents send you about sex, verbally and nonverbally?

_____

_____

13. How have the messages you received about sex affected you?

_____

_____

14. What did your father and mother think about men and women, and why?

_____

_____

15. Was your family religious? What part does religion play in your life today?

_____

_____

16. Was there much sickness in your family, and what did your mother and father do when someone got sick?

_____

_____

17. How do you act when your spouse is sick? How does your spouse act when you are sick?

_____

_____

18. When you were a child, who did the chores in the family?

_____

_____

19. Who does the chores in your family?

_____

_____

20. What did your parents do for fun?

_____

_____

21. What do you and your spouse do for fun?

_____

_____

22. Did your parents have a favorite motto or saying, and what was it?

_____

_____

23. How have these sayings or mottoes affected your life?

_____

_____

24. What did your parents praise you for when you were little?

_____

_____

25. What do you praise yourself for?

_____

_____

26. When things went wrong in your family, what feelings were your mother and father most likely to have—mad, sad, scared? How did you know your parents felt this way?

_____

_____

27. What is the feeling you are most likely to experience when things go wrong? What do you do to express this feeling?

_____

_____

28. Did you have any brothers or sisters? What was your relationship like with them?

_____

_____

29. Did you have a favorite childhood story, or hero, or radio or television show when you were a child? How do you think this affected your life?

_____

_____

30. What did your parents tell you about school and/or education?

_____

_____

31. How has what they said about school and education affected your life?

_____

_____

32. What did your father and mother want you to be when you grew up?

_____

_____

33. How have these messages affected your life?

_____

_____

34. When you were a child, what did you think was wrong with your father (physically, emotionally, socially)?

_____

_____

35. When you were a child, what did you think was wrong with your mother (physically, emotionally, socially)?

_____

_____

36. What did you think was wrong with you and why?

_____

_____

37. Is there anything that happened in your childhood that you think was especially significant? What was it?

_____

38. Is there anything that happened in your childhood that you think has affected your marriage significantly today? What was it?

_____

_____

39. If you could have changed anything about your parents' marriage when you were young, what would it have been?

_____

_____

40. If you could change anything about your marriage just by wishing, what would it be?

_____

_____

More Script Messages to Shake Your Memory

Below you'll probably see some of the messages you discovered while doing your Script Checklist. Check off the ones that apply to you.

- ☐ You're stupid.
- ☐ Be abandoned.
- ☐ Abandon people.
- ☐ Be a success.
- ☐ Be a failure.
- ☐ Men are passive.
- ☐ Women are passive.
- ☐ Don't grow up.
- ☐ Work before play.

- ☐ Sex is fun.
- ☐ Sex is dirty.
- ☐ Sex is for procreation.
- ☐ Don't think.
- ☐ Don't show your feelings.
- ☐ Get the job done.
- ☐ Be a decision maker.

- ☐ When things go wrong, go to bed.
- ☐ When things go wrong, take a pill.
- ☐ Be sexually abused.
- ☐ Don't get close.
- ☐ Live life to the fullest.

☐ Be affectionate.
☐ Don't be affection-
    ate.
☐ Be generous.
☐ Be selfish.
☐ Be responsible.
☐ Money is for
    spending.
☐ Be a miser.
☐ Have children.
☐ Be sexy.
☐ Women don't
    count.
☐ Be the black sheep.
☐ Kill yourself.
☐ Be lazy.
☐ You're a good
    child.
☐ Be like your
    mother.
☐ Be like your father.
☐ Don't compete.
☐ When things go
    wrong, drink.
☐ Be physically
    abused.
☐ Be the boss.
☐ Sex is not okay.

☐ Feel depressed.
☐ Be critical.
☐ Be angry.
☐ Hide your anger.
☐ Don't be sick.
☐ Be sick.
☐ Don't trust people.
☐ Be an abuser.
☐ Be considerate.
☐ Be sweet.
☐ Don't touch.
☐ You'll never find a
    woman.
☐ You'll never find a
    man.
☐ Play around.
☐ Depend on others.
☐ Women take care
    of you emotion-
    ally.
☐ You'll never
    amount to
    anything.

☐ Work hard.
☐ Women are
    bitches.
☐ Men are in charge.
☐ Women are in
    charge.
☐ Be perfect.
☐ Worry.
☐ Procrastinate.
☐ Be sarcastic.
☐ Enjoy life.
☐ Be religious.
☐ Go to church.
☐ Be a victim in life.
☐ Have a career.
☐ Be an alcoholic.
☐ Men are jerks.
☐ Be dumb.
☐ Be an achiever.
☐ You'll never find a
    job.
☐ Be a bum.
☐ Depend only on
    yourself.
☐ Men take care of
    you financially.
☐ Women are
    second-class
    citizens.
☐ You're no good.
☐ Be happy.

Your Script

Now write down all the messages that you have become aware of while reading through this chapter and doing the Script Checklist. These messages, then, are your script.

_____   _____

_____   _____

_____   _____

_____   _____

_____   _____

_____   _____

_____   _____

_____   _____

_____   _____

NO SCRIPT IS CARVED IN STONE

By reading this chapter and filling out the Script Checklist, you have come to understand more about how your childhood has affected your life and your marriage. In chapter 8, "Interlocking Scripts," I'll talk about what to do with your script now that you've identified it, and I'll show you how you can use your new understanding of yourself to help make your marriage better. But, for now, I just want you to remember one thing: No script is carved in stone.

Not everything you do today is based on what you learned in childhood, as you are constantly being bombarded with new information as to how you might live your life differently. In addition, you have gone through various experiences in your life which have made an impact on your script.

Consider, for example, the husband who has chosen to follow the script messages "Work hard," "Take life seriously," "Keep your nose to the grindstone," "Don't play," and "Don't share your thoughts and feelings." One day he is stricken with a debilitating illness. During his long period of recovery, he starts talking more with his wife. He becomes more attuned to his children and what is going on in their lives. He starts reading about the benefits of touch as part of the healing process. He starts laughing more at the little things in life. In the morning he sits and enjoys his coffee and watches the birds at the feeder. And slowly the messages he has chosen to follow all his life become less and less important. When he recovers and returns to work, he still does an excellent job, but now he is no longer so driven. His illness, his reading, and his period of convalescence have triggered in him an awareness that there are many things to enjoy besides a hard day's work. Truly he is a new man.

Another example is the woman who heard over and over again as a child, "You'll never amount to anything." For years she struggles against this message, but regardless of what she achieves, she still thinks she's worthless. Then one day she reads about herself in a prestigious publication and experiences an overwhelming feeling of self-worth. From that day on the message "You'll never amount to anything" no longer has power over her, and the need to defend against it by constant achievement is no longer necessary. Now she can take time for herself and pursue other things in life that are not tied to achievement.

Like these two people and Carolyn, whose Script Checklist you read earlier and who is busy reassessing her life, you have the final say-so over your script. You decide what messages you will follow and what messages you will discard. No one's script is all good, all bad, or carved in stone.

7

IT'S TIME FOR ANOTHER BREAK

When people discover their script, they often feel overwhelmed with sadness, hurt, or anger toward their parents for giving them such destructive messages. They can easily recall the pain that they had to go through or the pain they caused others as a result of these messages. When they reexperience some of these painful memories, they want to share their pain, sometimes with the very person who seems to have caused it. However, I ask you not to do this. If your parents gave you bad messages, accept that about them, and understand that it wasn't intentional.

One woman who focused on her childhood immediately went to her father and told him that the reason she was so messed up, and picked one man after another who didn't take care of her, was because *he* was never emotionally there for her as a child. This was clearly a game of If-It-Weren't-for-You, Dad. What she was forgetting is that *she* chose how she was going to follow that message, since she could have guarded against playing it out and carefully selected a man who would be there for her. In the end her confrontation caused both of them pain. And spreading her pain to her father didn't really help her. She now understands this, and wishes she hadn't acted so rashly.

Remember, too, you had some good messages from your parents; so don't forget to count them.

In order to take care of yourself, talk with your spouse about what you've learned, since talking will help you sort things out and will make you feel better. It will also bring the two of you closer because your spouse will now better understand why you act and often feel a certain way.

Also, give yourself a gold star for having the courage to look at your past.

8

INTERLOCKING SCRIPTS

YOUR SCRIPT AND YOUR MARRIAGE

Now that you're in touch with the script messages you received in childhood, you can start to see how you inadvertently play them out in your marriage and how you invite your spouse to help you play them out.

Acting Out the Messages

Here are some examples of how people act out various messages.

If a wife follows a script message from her childhood that says, "Be angry," she might try to do everything—cook, clean, work a full-time job, take care of all the children's and relatives' needs, and ask nothing of her husband. Then, periodically she might get fed up in order to justify being angry at everyone. If she takes on enough projects, she might justify being angry every day. If her husband has made the script decision that "women are bitches," he will let his wife do everything while he sits back, watches television, and listens to her bitch.

The spouse who has made the script decision to "feel trapped" might deprive herself of spending any money while encouraging her husband to buy everything he sees and wants. Or she might pull out the ledger she keeps in her head and review on a daily basis all the lousy things her husband has done in the past, playing the game If-It-Weren't-for-Him-I'd-Be-Happy.

A husband who has decided that "sex is not okay" may stay up at night working on his computer until his wife is asleep. Or he might refuse to approach her sexually, and when she approaches him, he might say he has indigestion from the rich dessert she made that night, shifting the responsibility to her for not having sex.

If a wife has made the decision that "laughter will cure anything," she may be able to see the humor in most things, easily forget yesterday's disappointments, laugh a lot, and generally enjoy life.

A wife who has decided to follow both the script messages "Be sexy" and "Sex is bad" may give her husband a sexy come-on in the afternoon, making suggestions of things to come, and by evening start picking fights to guarantee no sex that night. Or she may approach him sexually just as he's ready to leave the house for an important business meeting.

A man who has a script message "Go to church on Sunday" may never give himself permission to stay home from church on Sunday regardless of the fact that his temperature is 102 and he might spread his germs to others. Or he may get mad, throw a temper tantrum, and pout all day when his wife refuses to go to church with him, even though she does not share his convictions.

If a husband has a message to "work hard" and "enjoy life," he probably will work hard and play hard and enjoy whatever he is doing at the time he is doing it.

A husband who has decided to follow the message "Don't touch" is going to avoid physical contact with his wife. He won't voluntarily put his arm around his wife while they watch television. He won't initiate holding her hand, and when she takes his, he will pull away. And he won't be willing to snuggle in bed or be interested in much foreplay.

A wife who has a message "Work before play" is likely to work and never play, because she never gets everything quite finished. She may also refuse to leave on vacation with her husband until everything in the house is in perfect order, even though they might miss their airplane.

A husband who has made the script decision to "be generous" may shower his wife with presents, encourage her to spend money on herself, give lots of hugs, and be conscious of his wife's enjoyment when they make love.

The wife following the script "Be abandoned" is likely to do all sorts of provocative things to get her husband to leave her, either emotionally or physically. She might gripe all the time, look like a mess, or walk around feeling sad and depressed. Or she may flip the message over, have an affair, and leave him.

The wife who has the message "Take care of others" will always be taking the emotional temperature of those around her so she can make them feel good. In addition, she will try to meet their physical needs by doing everything for everyone: She will be a friend, lover, confidante, nurse, secretary, laundress, chauffeur, housekeeper, baker, and breadwinner.

A husband who believes that "women are second-class citizens" will feel justified in meeting his needs first. He won't call when he's going to be late. He won't give his wife a Valentine's Day present because he doesn't believe in that nonsense, even though she has repeatedly said such gifts mean a lot to her. He'll be stingy with compliments, he'll give presents that he likes instead of considering what she likes, he'll only have sex when he wants it, and he'll spend more on himself than on his wife.

A wife with the message "Touching is okay" is likely to give her husband lots of hugs and kisses, reach out and take his hand when they're talking, rumple his hair, and brush against him when they pass each other in the house.

A husband with the script message "People are trustworthy" will most probably be loyal to his wife, not get involved with other women, be up-front with what he spends, and never reveal secrets his wife has shared with him.

The wife with the script message "Be a victim" is likely to stay married to a man who refuses to get a job, abuses her physically, or calls her every name in the book whenever he pleases.

A husband who has the script message "Men are not dependable" may cheat on his wife every chance he gets, visit her only occasionally when she's in the hospital, refuse to talk when they have guests for the evening, and tell everyone at the office about her performance in bed.

Once again, it becomes clear how one's script decision can affect a marriage, day in, day out.

Meshing Scripts

Because your spouse also has a script that he or she is busy following, you will want to be cognizant of how the two of you have meshed your scripts over the years. To understand what I mean by "meshing your scripts," take a look at the following examples.

● Joe and Martha

This scene takes place in the evening. Joe comes home from work and goes directly to the bedroom to change his clothes. On hearing him, Martha stops what she's doing and goes to the bedroom. She walks over to him, greets him with a kiss to which he responds only halfheartedly, and then she sits on the bed and asks how his day was.

He tells her briefly what went on and starts to walk to the kitchen to get the mail. Martha follows him, and without his asking she tells him about her day. As she talks he thumbs through the mail and does not look at her. When she asks him about his cold, he says, "It's still here," which throws up an immediate barrier to the concern she has shown for him. Later in the evening he goes out for cigarettes and fails to tell her he's leaving the house. She finds out he's gone when someone telephones and she can't find him anywhere around. That night, as they're getting ready for bed and she's telling him about their son's day in school, he walks into the bathroom. She follows him and continues to talk as he brushes his teeth. Finally, after getting into bed, Martha leans over and gives him a kiss and a hug, and he gives her a pat on the arm. He has played out "Don't be close," and she has played out "Try hard."

● Rosalie and Bart

I remember working with one woman in therapy whose script read "Men leave you." Rosalie's father was an alcoholic, her first husband didn't drink but he was a workaholic, and her present husband, Bart, was "nice" but "too quiet." All three acted differently, but they had one thing in common: They all abandoned Rosalie emotionally. The alcoholic father was always "out of it" and wasn't able to provide the emotional warmth she required. The workaholic husband was never there, and when he was with her, he continued to focus on his work. Bart was passive and did not provide her with the emotional warmth she craved. Both husbands helped her play out her script "Men leave you," while they played out their own message, "Don't be close."

● Cindy and Mike

Cindy and Mike, another couple I saw in marriage counseling, also had script messages that fit perfectly . . . but unfortunately in a destructive manner.

Cindy's family gave her almost anything she wanted when she was growing up. If there wasn't enough money to pay for something, Cindy's mother would figure out a way to get it for her. Cindy's parents constantly fought about the money that her mother spent. Cindy's grandmother also played a part in the drama, because she would slip Cindy and her mother additional money. Cindy's script messages included "I deserve it," "Be sneaky," and "Overspend."

Mike's parents believed "people take advantage of others" and "everyone is in it for themselves," phrases they frequently quoted to him. We traced these messages back to when Mike's grandfather lost his company because of a cousin's fancy legal paperwork. When Mike did anything that was considered inappropriate, his father would overreact and scream that even Mike was out to take advantage of him. Mike's messages included "People can't be trusted," "Watch your money," "Be critical," "Be criticized by others," and "Have a temper."

It's obvious why Cindy and Mike's problems often centered around money. In their mutually destructive scenarios, Act I called for Cindy to overspend and then hide the bills. In Act II Cindy would 'fess up to her shenanigans because she couldn't pay the bills herself. When she did confess, Mike would confirm for himself that people can't be trusted. He would start lecturing Cindy about her spending. Cindy in turn would accuse Mike of being a penny pincher. Finally, in Act III Mike would have a temper tantrum, culminating in slamming the front door, going to a bar, and drinking too much.

● David and Allison

David and Allison also had meshed their script lines, causing emotional pain for both of them.

When David was born, his parents were in their early forties. His closest siblings were his twelve-year-old twin sisters. As far back as David could remember, he got his own way; "My parents were ready to stop raising kids and they were too tired to discipline me," he recalled. When David was seven years old, he had a teacher he "hated," and he started refusing to go to school. So his mother let him stay home. If she did push him to go, he would lie down on the living room floor and have a temper tantrum, which he immediately stopped when his mother said, "All right, you can stay home today."

By the time David got married, he was pretty used to doing just what he wanted. He had a poor job history because whenever he didn't feel like going to work, he didn't. Each day he lived out the script message "Do what you want."

David's wife, Allison, was raised in a family where her mother played peacemaker and was passive, while her father played tyrant. When Allison did something that her father did not approve of, he would "go crazy" and punish her inappropriately. For not using correct table manners, for example, Allison was forced to sit on the floor and eat out of the cat's dish; this was supposed to teach Allison better table manners.

Allison's script messages included "Be passive" (with a father like hers, she wouldn't have dared to protest) and "Men are tyrants."

It's no wonder David and Allison found each other attractive and saw the potential for carrying out their script messages.

I still remember the first time I saw them. They were in a real crisis over David's not getting up and going to work. If Allison woke David in the morning, he would be furious. He wouldn't talk to her, and because she woke him up, he justified doing as he pleased: not going to work, not coming home until all hours of the night, getting drunk, and not helping Allison with the children.

On the other hand, if Allison did not wake David up, he would be equally furious at her. He refused to talk to her, and he used her *not* waking him to justify doing what he pleased: not going to work, not coming home until all hours of the night, getting drunk, and not helping Allison with the children.

The old Corner game was in full swing, and both spouses were playing out their script messages. David played "I'll do what I please," and Allison played "Men are tyrants."

● Jim and Barbara

When I saw Jim and Barbara in marriage counseling, we figured out some of their script messages and it became instantly clear how their script lines fit together.

Jim came from a family of three boys. Jim's father, an ex—army drill sergeant, handled his family the same way he dealt with the recruits in boot camp: He continually told his sons what to do and how to do it, trying to get them to "shape up." Unable to defend himself against his father's constant barrage of criticism and lengthy lectures, Jim learned to sit still, look at his father, and not hear a word he said. Blocking out was Jim's way of protecting himself. Jim's script said, "Shape up," "Be criticized by others," and "Be picked on unjustly."

Barbara, Jim's wife, grew up in a family with no man around. Her father had deserted the family when Barbara was two years old, and she had no contact with him until she was twenty-four, when she hired a detective service to locate him so she could "at least see what he looked like." As a child, all Barbara heard from her mother was that her father was a no-good rat. In addition, Barbara's mother and two older sisters got involved with one no-good rat after another. Barbara's script contained the lines "Be discounted by men," "Be critical of men," and "Men are no good."

The way this couple played their script lines was that Jim would do something annoying, such as not calling Barbara to let her know he was working late, which set the stage for Barbara to be critical of Jim. When Jim came home, Barbara would say, "Couldn't you at least have called?" This would allow Jim to feel picked on and be able to reexperience past feelings from childhood. He then would defend his behavior, which allowed Barbara to feel discounted. She in turn would move to the script line she had heard so often in childhood: "All men are alike—no-good rats." Jim, feeling picked on, would tune out, take a trip in his head, and thus invite further criticism. Barbara at this point would escalate her anger to get through to Jim.

No matter what Barbara and Jim fought about, the result always seemed to be the same: Jim would be criticized, feel picked on unjustly, and tune out. Barbara would feel discounted, be critical, and reaffirm that men are no good. Their script lines fit perfectly.

It's Up to You

Not all script lines are bad, and many couples don't play them out as destructively as the couples I mentioned. At the same time, most couples play out some destructive messages, and it is these messages you must guard against if you want a good marriage. Take Jim, for example. In counseling, he made an agreement to come home on time. If he found he was going to be late, he called Barbara. When he messed up in other areas, he apologized. With these changes in behavior, Barbara no longer got so angry with him. Nor did she move to her script line "Men are no good," which in turn prevented Jim from moving to his script lines "Be criticized by others" and "Be picked on unjustly." He changed his script, his wife changed hers, and their marriage got better.

PLAYING OUT THE SCRIPTS IN *YOUR* MARRIAGE

Now it's time to figure out how you and your mate mesh your script lines. If your mate is willing, ask him or her to join you in doing this exercise. If you don't do it together, simply write down what you think your mate's script messages might be. Write down three messages from your script and three messages from your mate's script.

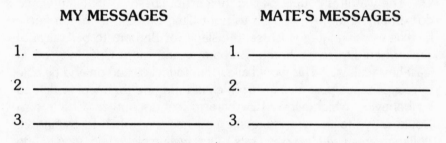

MY MESSAGES   **MATE'S MESSAGES**

1. _____   1. _____

2. _____   2. _____

3. _____   3. _____

Can you see how the two of you help each other play out these lines? Interesting, yes? If you don't like what you see, decide to change some of your behavior. As you change your behavior, you change your script, and your mate changes his. Or, as you change, your marriage changes.

9

SCRIPT POSITIONS

WHO ARE YOU?

As you follow the script messages you learned in childhood, you are unconsciously falling into certain behavior patterns. These behavior patterns ultimately lead you to assume a particular script position* in your marriage.

The four main positions that people generally occupy in their marriages are Caretaker, Passive Taker, Corrector, and Passive Aggressive. Almost everyone falls into one of these categories and behaves accordingly. Occasionally, however, a person will switch back and forth between two of these positions.

The problem with all of these positions is that they are destructive to the individuals who get caught in playing them out. They represent extremes in behavior. They cause tremendous problems in a relationship. And they play a significant part in the breakup of most marriages. Therefore, it's vital to know what position you are in, what position your spouse is in, what each of you specifically do to perpetuate these positions, and how you can extricate yourself from them.

Caretaker

Caretakers are people who almost always put their mate's needs ahead of their own. Because they are forever focused on their partner, their intuitive powers are highly developed. They use their intuition to "psych out" what's going on with their mate; they can walk into a room and "know" what their spouse is feeling. If their spouse is feeling happy, they feel happy. If their spouse feels down in the dumps, they become agitated and try every tactic they know to make their mate feel better. They cannot feel good unless their mate feels good. It's as if their mate is an extension of themselves and their very happiness depends on their mate's happiness. To some extent this is true, since Caretakers have been scripted to take care of others, both physically and emotionally. And when they feel they're not doing their job, they become increasingly anxious.

Usually Caretakers are women, because in our society girls most often are scripted to take care of others' emotional needs. The child who has been chosen by her family to be the Caretaker is often given too much responsibility at too young an age. Regardless of the inappropriateness of her family's expectations, the young Caretaker does what is expected. I know Caretakers who, when they were nine years old, were already washing, ironing, dusting, vacuuming, cooking, and baby-sitting one or two younger siblings.

Taking care of others was what the child did day in, day out, so this behavior became a way of life. The Caretaker child often was complimented for her caretaking abilities, thus reinforcing this behavior pattern. "You're such a good little girl for taking care of baby brother" and "You're so sweet for doing all the dishes" became the strokes that helped cast the die. Soon the child became dependent on this kind of recognition. In order to get this same recognition later in life, she had to continue taking care of others. When it was time to select a mate, Caretaker chose someone she could take care of.

A Caretaker's script includes these messages "Take care of others," "Be aware of others' feelings," "Others come first," "Be perfect," "Work hard," "Be responsible," "Get the job done," "Feel what's going on," and "Put others' wants and needs ahead of your own." Most Caretakers also have heard a few thousand times, "Idle hands are the devil's workshop," "Anything worth doing is worth doing well," and "Work before play."

When given one compliment, Caretakers give five back. They have trouble feeling and hearing the strokes of others, however, because they often are not in touch with their own feelings. The strokes they do hear and accept are conditional; that is, Caretakers believe that they must have done something to be worthy of receiving a stroke. Internally they do a fair amount of conditional self-stroking, such as,

"I'm a good person for picking up his clothes," and, "I'm a nice person for washing the car." This conditional internal stroking serves to keep them locked into the Caretaker position. They also continue to script themselves to caretake by saying, "Who will do it if I don't?" and, "Things would fall apart around here if I didn't do it." Primarily they give themselves strokes when they are doing what they have been scripted to do. These strokes keep them even more locked into their position.

A Caretaker also tends to be an advice giver, and others seek her out for this reason. When *she* has a problem, however, she is reluctant to ask for help. Also, her spouse often discourages her from sharing her feelings and asking for help with such statements as, "Oh, you'll feel better tomorrow," or, "Don't worry, everything will work out." These perfunctory statements are designed to keep Caretaker from focusing on herself and her needs.

Not long ago, after giving a talk on marriage, I was leaving the auditorium and a woman came up and told me, rather proudly, that she had laid out her husband's clothes, including his underwear, for the past thirty years. And she was smiling! Personally, I thought it was a little much. My tolerance for the woman instantly grew, however, when I remembered that for the first ten years of my marriage, I had fixed not only the children's sandwiches and my own, but my husband's as well. We would sit around the kitchen table and I would prepare his sandwich—"Mayonnaise? . . . Mustard? . . . Lettuce? . . . Tomato?"—and then I would cut it in two before I handed it to him.

It wasn't until another person pointed this out to me by saying, "You fix *his* sandwich, too!" that I could see what I was doing and realized that he could fix his own sandwich—which, incidentally, he was perfectly willing to do. He also didn't mind letting me fix his sandwich, because his mother had done it for him. It was part of my script to wait on a man, and it was part of his script to be waited on by a woman. So neither of us thought to question my fixing his sandwich. The problem, of course, was not fixing his sandwich, which is nice to do for someone, but our blind acceptance of my doing it because this is what I was supposed to do. (It is important not to confuse the Caretaker position with the spouse who makes a deliberate decision to do something nice for her mate, taking into account both her needs and those of others. The Caretaker position should also not be confused with the "caretaker professions," such as doctors, nurses, psychotherapists, social workers, child-care workers, and the clergy.)

The position of Caretaker automatically gives a person tremendous power in the marriage, since a Caretaker makes most of the decisions. She enjoys this position of power, but at the same time she often feels cheated because her spouse doesn't take more responsibility and make more decisions in the relationship. When her spouse tries to take more responsibility, however, the Caretaker is right there trying to take charge once again.

● Typical Caretaker Behaviors

Here are some typical examples of a Caretaker in action:

—Caretaker goes out of town on business. Before she goes, she cooks and freezes every meal, lays out everyone's clothes, leaves elaborate instruction sheets taped on every mirror and door, and then she calls every night while she's away with additional instructions so everything goes smoothly.

—Caretaker's husband spills red wine all over a friend's living room rug. Caretaker comes home, checks their homeowner's policy, calls the insurance company, calls three rug-cleaning services and makes arrangements with one of them, coordinates with the friend when the rug-cleaning service will come, and sends a note of apology.

—It's time for vacation. Caretaker, who has a full-time job, makes the reservations; runs to the travel agent to pick up maps; has the oil changed and the wheels balanced; gets the suitcases down from the attic; washes, irons, and packs everyone's clothes; takes the children shopping for a few extra outfits; makes arrangements with the kennel; has the newspaper and mail stopped; hires the boy next door to water the plants; goes to the bank and gets the traveler's checks; leaves emergency phone numbers with several relatives; gets the car washed; buys snacks to take along on the trip; runs to the dime store for crayons and coloring books so the children will have something to do in the back seat; and then packs the car.

● The Caretaker Test

If you are a Caretaker, you probably have recognized yourself already. But if you have any doubt, go through the following Caretaker Test and mark the boxes that apply to you.

☐ **1.** You are constantly concerned about your spouse's mood, forever taking his emotional temperature, and feel responsible when your spouse is depressed, bored, angry, sad, or unhappy.

☐ **2.** You are *more aware* of your spouse's feelings than your own.

☐ **3.** You give compliments, hugs, pats on the back, and presents, and you *always* try to please.

☐ **4.** You prepare well in advance for birthdays, holidays, vacations, and social gatherings so everything will be just right.

☐ **5.** You are willing to drop your own plans for those of your spouse at a moment's notice.

☐ **6.** You have a high energy level, you are ambitious and definitely a doer in life.

☐ **7.** You have the ability to look at a situation and recognize instantly what needs to be done.

☐ **8.** You have trouble relaxing, and when you do, you still work on little projects such as paying the bills while watching television or wiping off the kitchen cabinets while talking to a friend on the telephone.

☐ **9.** You are well organized, efficient, and somewhat compulsive.

☐ **10.** You secretly enjoy taking charge and making sure things get done.

Do you qualify?

If you have checked eight or more characteristics, you are definitely a Caretaker. If you have checked five to seven, you sometimes are in the Caretaker position.

Passive Taker

Passive Takers are people who are only vaguely aware of their wants and needs and what they like and dislike. They rarely feel strongly about anything. Their lot in life is to accept what's happening to them at that time. Perhaps the best description is that they allow themselves to float along without focusing on what they want and what is going on around them. They passively take what is dealt them in life and do not think to question that they have a choice, or that they can make any impact on their life. Passive Takers are middle-of-the-road and usually even-tempered.

As children, Passive Takers were taught to expect others to take care of them. Often they had a parent, grandparent, aunt, or sibling who was their assigned Caretaker. They were expected to do what they were told, but expectations were usually minimal. With their wants consistently taken care of, they didn't learn to plan ahead or think about what they wanted, nor did they learn to focus on anyone else's needs. Focusing on their own or their spouse's wants and needs is not part of their frame of reference. They simply never learned how to do it.

Passive Takers are usually men who, as boys, were scripted to expect to be taken care of by women. Their script messages include "Other people will take care of you," "Don't think too much," "Don't feel too much," "Don't worry too much," "Take it easy," "Be accepting," and "Don't rock the boat." They also heard a few thousand times, "Take life as it comes," and, "Live day to day."

Passive Takers do not initiate or organize in the marriage. They complacently go along with the program, but they never take charge and plan it. They are willing to help, but chores must be assigned. They rarely are aware of what their spouse likes and dislikes, nor are they aware of her feelings. They do not compliment their spouse, nor do they criticize. Perhaps their major flaw is that they do not think about their own wants or try to meet their spouse's needs and wants. They do not anticipate or see what should be done.

I want to emphasize that a Passive Taker does not think in the same way other people think. He does not come home and say to himself, "I'm going to watch the football game tonight and the heck with what my spouse wants." He simply doesn't think about what he or his spouse will be doing. He comes home from work, clicks on the television, sees that a football game is in progress, and settles in to watch it. What his spouse happens to be doing does not cross his mind. Passive Takers are not the opposite of Caretakers; they operate from their own frame of reference, which is a different frame of reference from that of the Caretaker.

● Typical Passive Taker Behaviors

Here are some typical examples of the behavior of a Passive Taker:

—Mate asks Passive Taker what he would like for dinner; Passive Taker responds, "Anything."

—Wife asks Passive Taker if he plans to go to the boys' soccer game on Saturday; he says, "I hadn't thought about it."

—Mate asks Passive Taker what he plans to wear to the dinner dance Saturday night; he says, "You decide."

—Wife asks Passive Taker what movie he would like to see; he responds, "It doesn't matter."

In fact, it doesn't matter if mate buys a new microwave oven, has her ears pierced, colors her hair, or loses fifty pounds. Passive Taker's response is, "Whatever."

● The Passive Taker Test

This test can help you determine if you are a Passive Taker. Check off those characteristics that apply to you.

☐ **1.** You will help out if assigned a task, like setting the table or putting away the suitcases, but you rarely take the initiative and do these things yourself or start a project on your own.

☐ **2.** You are content doing almost anything, spend most of your free time alone, live in your own world, and do not have a need to interact with others.

☐ **3.** You rarely ask your spouse to do something for you. You make few demands.

☐ **4.** You do not think in advance or plan ahead in your marriage. You do not shop more than a day or two ahead for birthdays, or call ahead for reservations, or think in terms of the future.

☐ **5.** You are not attuned to the wants or feelings of your spouse.

☐ **6.** You rarely give compliments or pats on the back, nor do you "see" what your spouse has done for you.

☐ **7.** You are rarely critical of yourself or your spouse.

☐ **8.** You are viewed by the outside world as nice, easygoing, and content.

☐ **9.** You are often accused by your spouse of being selfish and lazy and are told, "You just don't care."

☐ **10.** You are noncompetitive and prefer to let others take the lead.

Do you qualify?

If you have checked eight or more characteristics, you are definitely a Passive Taker. If you have checked five to seven, you sometimes exhibit Passive Taker behaviors.

Corrector

Persons who take the position of Corrector in the marriage are forever finding fault with someone or something. They can take the best-looking suit, the nicest dinner, or the neatest party and invariably see something wrong with it. Their primary focus is to find the flaw.

Usually one or both parents of Correctors were overly critical. Consequently, these children came to develop an overly critical attitude about life. Correctors expect perfection. Rarely are they satisfied with their own performance, and they constantly put themselves down for what they did or didn't do. If they do ten things right and one thing wrong, it's what they did wrong that becomes the focus of their attention. This negativism spills over to the way they perceive the world and everyone in it, and often their spouse becomes the target of their criticism.

Internally, a Corrector is driven by messages received in childhood such as "Be perfect," "Do it right," "Toe the mark," "Work hard," and "Be responsible." Other messages include "Be critical," "Be criticized by others," "Don't count your chickens before they're hatched," and "If you think it's bad now, just you wait." The Corrector position is shared equally by men and women.

As with the Caretaker, the Corrector likes to call the shots and tell others what to do and how to do it. He or she enjoys being in a position of control. Instead of taking control by first looking over a situation that needs changing and then doing something about it (as the Caretaker would), the Corrector tries to control by criticizing his spouse into doing something about the problem.

Correctors tend to be organized, opinionated, somewhat stingy, and often boring. They enjoy giving advice, much of which is in the form of platitudes and clichés. Correctors use "always" and "never" when trying to get a point across, as well as "Why don't you," "Why did you," "How come you don't," "You ought to," and "You should." In addition, they have a habit of wagging their pointer finger when talking. Because they have such a need to be in control of everything, they usually lack spontaneity. Most of their play time is structured, and often the "right" way to do something becomes the focus. For the Corrector, there is a "right" way to fold socks, a "right" way to mow the lawn, and a "right" way to catch a fish.

● Typical Corrector Behaviors

Here are some typical examples of the behavior of a Corrector:

—Husband is washing the dishes; Corrector walks over to the sink, reaches around him, and turns down the water.

—Wife is cooking dinner; Corrector says, "Say, do we need all these lights on just to cook dinner? Money doesn't grow on trees, you know."

—Husband hangs up the towels in the bathroom; Corrector comes along and rehangs them.

—Wife is getting ready for a party, looks at herself in the mirror, and says, "Gee, I sure like this dress"; Corrector says, "I don't think it flatters you as much as some of your other dresses."

● The Corrector Test

People who are in the position of Corrector in their marriage often have difficulty seeing themselves in this light, perhaps because they have trouble accepting, or "owning,"* that this is the way they generally behave. Take the following Corrector Test to see if you qualify. Check each item that applies to you.

☐ **1.** You are overly critical of yourself for things you did or didn't do. You mentally review your performance.

☐ **2.** You are overly critical of your spouse and quick to point out his or her flaws. Off the top of your head you could easily name a number of tasks your spouse does wrong.

☐ **3.** You continually strive to be perfect and consider yourself a perfectionist.

☐ **4.** You tend to define the world in terms of black and white, right and wrong, good and bad. Your thinking is often polarized. Once you have made a decision, you have trouble understanding or accepting the other person's point of view.

☐ **5.** You are selfish with giving compliments and often are accused of being sexually selfish. You may or may not be selfish with your money.

☐ **6.** You use anger, and various forms of anger such as put-downs, sarcasm, guilt, or pouting, to intimidate and control your spouse and to get your own way.

☐ **7.** You enjoy telling your mate what to do, and you get a feeling of satisfaction when you explain how to do it.

☐ **8.** You schedule "free-time" activities carefully to get the most out of your time and rarely engage in spontaneous play. Your fun usually has a purpose.

☐ **9.** You are well organized, efficient, and accomplish a good deal both at work and at home.

☐ **10.** You think of yourself as someone who can be counted on, is loyal, and keeps his word.

Do you qualify?

If you have checked eight or more characteristics, you are definitely a Corrector. If you have checked five to seven, you sometimes are in the Corrector position.

Passive Aggressive

Passive Aggressives operate from a center-of-the-world, "I count more than you count," position, which translates into behaviors that continually discount others. Passive Aggressives do what they want to do, not because they don't care about others (many are quite sensitive), but because they follow their *own* standards of behavior. They often are late, and they procrastinate, and forget, and generally achieve less than they are capable of. They could get the job done faster and better, but they don't.

The first script messages the Passive Aggressive receives in childhood include "You're special," "Do it right," "Be perfect," "Work hard," "Achieve," and "Be a success." These messages are similar to those received by the Caretaker. As time goes on, however, the child starts hearing, "When are you going to do it right?", "Can't you ever get the job done correctly?", "You'll never amount to anything," "When will you ever grow up?", and, "You're a mess-up." Also, because of the constant criticism the child receives, he internalizes the messages "Be criticized" and "Be critical." And since most of these messages are delivered in an angry fashion, he also internalizes the message "Be angry." The Passive Aggressive position is shared equally by men and women.

In essence, the Passive Aggressive's everyday behavior is angry because he doesn't adapt to the same standards as others and his behavior therefore discounts others. His anger simply is expressed in a passive manner. His spouse, on the other hand, often feels angry because his behavior impinges on her life; and in time she expresses the anger openly. Thus you might say the Passive Aggressive passes his anger to his spouse, and she expresses it for him.

This is not to say the Passive Aggressive is not capable of expressing anger openly. In addition to passively expressing anger, the Passive Aggressive often has a bad temper and frequently loses it when challenged on his behavior or when things don't go exactly his way. These angry explosions often cause his spouse and others to treat him gingerly and give him more latitude than someone else would receive. The Passive Aggressive's belief that he counts more than others is again reinforced.

Passive Aggressives are usually emotionally dependent on their spouses because they have never completely disengaged from the power struggle of childhood, which took the form of the parent saying, "Do it right," and the Passive Aggressive "not quite doing it right" or "not quite doing it." Most often they choose a spouse who is efficient and knows how to get the job done. Passive Aggressives secretly resent their spouse's efficiency, although this resentment is rarely on a conscious level.

One interesting and definitely exasperating dynamic that occurs when you deal with a Passive Aggressive mate is that you often wind up feeling aggressive yourself. The Passive Aggressive is late, and you feel angry. She forgets to pay the house payment, and you feel angry. He leaves his shoes in the middle of the room exactly where he takes them off, and you feel angry. He feels innocent and looks like a nice guy who simply "forgot," while you "go nuts" and look ridiculous.

The spouse of a Passive Aggressive is often angry and feels as though she deserves an apology. Because a Passive Aggressive sees himself as innocent of any wrongdoing, he rarely apologizes, or he apologizes as a maneuver to appease his mate. Unlike most apologies, however, the Passive Aggressive's apology does not contain a promise to change. And that's why the next day, or the next week, he turns around and commits the very same offense again.

● Typical Passive Aggressive Behaviors

Here are some everyday examples of Passive Aggressive's behavior:

—It's raining, and Passive Aggressive finds that he has left his umbrella at the office. So he takes his wife's umbrella from the closet, even though she, too, is going to be leaving the house in the next few minutes.

—Passive Aggressive decides to tape a movie on the videocassette recorder. She can't find a blank tape, so she takes one of her husband's and tapes over a World Series game he has been saving for the past four years.

—Wife is listening to an old comedy routine on the radio and laughing uproariously; Passive Aggressive walks over and changes the station to the ball game.

—Passive Aggressive goes to her husband's wallet and takes money for lunch without telling him. When husband goes to pay for his lunch, he finds he has no money.

—Passive Aggressive uses her husband's car and leaves dirty tissues, an empty soda can, a banana peel on the floor, and the gas tank on empty.

—Passive Aggressive says he'll pay the electric bill, tucks it in his coat pocket, and forgets about it entirely.

● The Passive Aggressive Test

You may not know that you are a Passive Aggressive; many people are not aware that they are in this position. Take the following test to determine if you are a Passive Aggressive. Check off those characteristics that apply to you.

☐ 1. You do what you want to do, when you want to do it, and how you want to do it. You set your own standards of behavior as opposed to following the standards of others.

☐ 2. You resist expectations of others by dawdling and forgetting. You hate it when others set deadlines for you and often you do not meet them.

☐ 3. You get angry when crossed; you have a nasty temper and frequently use it to try to make your point, intimidate, and get your own way.

☐ 4. You think others have no right to tell you what to do, and often when you are told what to do you respond in a defensive and hostile manner.

☐ 5. You rarely find yourself in a position where you think you have made a mistake and you need to apologize.

☐ 6. You often do not do what you have promised, and your spouse is always on you about what you haven't done.

☐ 7. You are unsure of yourself, and internally you feel powerless and dependent and lack self-confidence.

☐ 8. You defend your behavior with such excuses as "I forgot," "It never occurred to me," or "I'm sorry you think that of me." You feel innocent when you offer these excuses, and when you apologize it is usually a maneuver to get your spouse off your case. Your apologies do not contain a promise to change.

☐ 9. You don't think about how your behavior affects others. You simply do not take others' wants and feelings into account if you want to do something.

☐ 10. You see yourself as basically a nice person and can't understand why others often feel irritated and angry with you.

Do you qualify?

If you have checked eight or more characteristics, you are definitely a Passive Aggressive. If you have checked five to seven, you sometimes exhibit Passive Aggressive behavior.

BEYOND THE FOUR PRIMARY POSITIONS

After taking these tests, you may have found that you qualify for more than one of the primary script positions. This is because the positions are not mutually exclusive. It's possible to operate part of the time in one position and part of the time in another.

For example, a Caretaker may continually take her husband's emotional temperature, be unaware of her own feelings, give her husband a constant stream of compliments, place his wants above her own, always see what should be done, prepare well in advance for all events, efficiently follow through, and have difficulty relaxing. She may *also* be overly critical of herself and her spouse, use anger to try to intimidate him, have trouble acting silly and playing, and constantly tell her husband what to do.

This, incidentally, is the reason why many Caretakers seem a little off-balance emotionally. One day they are busy doing everything for their spouse and "loving it" (Caretaker), and the next day they are feeling gypped, and are focusing on what their spouse didn't do (Corrector).

A Caretaker moves so easily to a Corrector because some of the script messages of these two positions are similar. For example, both are well organized, efficient, and get the job done. Both are taught to focus outward on something other than themselves. A Caretaker focuses on their spouse's emotional well-being; a Corrector focuses on their spouse's flaws.

After interviewing hundreds of Caretakers, I've found that this change in focus tends to take place as the person assumes more responsibilities. Initially she may be exclusively a Caretaker. But at some point, when she's overextended and she feels overwhelmed with all she has to do, she switches the focus to her husband's flaws. This focus allows her to justify not taking care of him. Because she remains highly intuitive and always knows what's going on with him emotionally, and because she continues to believe that her job is to please, she switches back to Caretaker whenever she has time and energy to give to him.

The Passive Taker will never share the position of Caretaker, Corrector, or Passive Aggressive. However, some Passive Takers have behaviors that are similar to those of the Passive Aggressive. For instance, both tend to operate at a lower level of efficiency than they are capable of. The Passive Aggressive chooses this lower level of efficiency because a certain task is not a priority with him at that particular time. A Passive Taker operates from a lower level of efficiency because he's passive and doesn't think about how the task could be done more efficiently. The Passive Aggressive's focus is himself and what he wants. The Passive Taker has no focus and doesn't think about what he wants or what someone else wants.

A Corrector may share the position of Caretaker, since they share some common script messages, but this switching of positions does not occur frequently. Although the Corrector gets the job done and done correctly, he does not continually "feel" where his wife is emotionally, nor does he operate from the frame of reference of placing his wife's needs above his own. He might do something she wants as opposed to what he wants, and he may be aware of how she is feeling from time to time, but he does not continually take her emotional temperature.

The Passive Aggressive by very definition does what he wants to do, and therefore he does not move into another position. He may have characteristics of the Caretaker, Corrector, and Passive Taker, but his position is Passive Aggressive. That's why in the evening he insists on doing the dishes for his wife (he wants to help her), and the next day he breaks his lunch date with her (he wants to play golf). And then that night, as they are discussing movies, he is noncommittal about what he wants to see (he doesn't want to make a decision), so he leaves the decision to her.

The Angry Righteous and Rebellious Positions

In addition to the four primary script positions there are two secondary positions:* the Angry Righteous* position and the Rebellious* position. These positions are in response to a spouse's inappropriate behavior and they are used infrequently. Often, one's behavior while in one of these secondary positions is inconsistent with the characteristics of his primary position.

A person is likely to shift into the Angry Righteous position of "How dare he!" or "How dare she!" in response to feeling extremely trod on, or trod on one too many times in a relationship. While in the Angry Righteous position, the person feels intense anger. This anger allows him to justify behaving differently than he is accustomed to because normally his script does not allow for this type of behavior.

For example, Corrector and his wife have agreed on a certain budget, and while Corrector forfeits what he wants to buy, his Passive Aggressive wife continually goes off the budget and does what she wants. When the Corrector husband finds out that his Passive Aggressive wife has purchased a $250 snakeskin wallet that they cannot afford, he moves to Angry Righteous and refuses to talk to her for the next two days. His silence is in response to his wife's Passive Aggressive behavior.

Another example is the Caretaker wife who throws a surprise party for her husband's fortieth birthday. Two months later her Passive Aggressive husband forgets her birthday entirely and makes plans to go hunting. When the wife finds out that Passive Aggressive husband "did not *even remember my birthday!*" she moves to the Angry Righteous position and tells her husband off in no uncertain terms. And for a time she feels justified in not taking care of him. This behavior is a response to her husband's grossly neglectful behavior.

A person may shift to the Rebellious position of "How dare he tell me what to do!" or "How dare she criticize me!" in response to the spouse's attempt at control. An example is the Passive Aggressive wife who starts any number of projects around the house and never finishes any of them. After Corrector husband presents her with a time-management chart for how she can get her projects finished, she moves to the position of Rebellious, digs in her heels, and thinks, "Nobody is going to tell me how to run my house!" For a few days she refuses to do *anything.* When her anger subsides, she resumes her Passive Aggressive position of doing things around the house on her terms and at her own Passive Aggressive pace.

Although a Passive Aggressive does not move from one primary position to another, a Passive Aggressive may move to the secondary position of Rebellious. This happens when someone else tries to put parameters on her behavior. In the above example, the Passive Aggressive still does what she wants, but now her doing what she wants is in response to her husband. You might say the Rebellious position is an extreme of the Passive Aggressive position.

While both the Angry Righteous and the Rebellious positions appear similar, Angry Righteous comes from the indignation that a person feels toward others when they do not act responsibly. In the Rebellious position, however, a person feels indignant when someone else dares to infringe on his behavior and his way of doing things. This is why Caretakers and Correctors are more likely to shift to Angry

Righteous, because they're responsible individuals and expect other people to be responsible as well. Passive Aggressives and Passive Takers, on the other hand, are more likely to shift to Rebellious, because they're used to doing what they please.

Your Family and Your Script Position

It seems that the overriding factors for determining what script messages you received and the ultimate script position you take is based on (1) your parents' script position, (2) what role they subconsciously needed you to be in, (3) whether you are male or female, and (4) the age and sex of your siblings.

For instance, if the mother is a Caretaker, scoring eight or more points on the Caretaker Test, and the father is a Passive Taker, scoring eight or more points on the Passive Taker Test, their first child probably will become a Passive Aggressive, particularly if the child is male.

The reason is that the Caretaker mother is young and energetic, and she expects perfection—not only from herself but from her child as well. She scrutinizes everything her son does, and because children are less than perfect, the mother finds a lot of areas where her son needs improvement. She is forever telling him, "Do it this way," or, "You're doing it wrong." The Caretaker mother wants her son to be perfect and to have a perfect life.

On the other hand, the Passive Taker father is busy with his own career, so he does not take much time with this child, nor does he become very emotionally involved. The father is simply physically there some of the time. Also, because the father doesn't know much about child rearing and isn't particularly interested, he goes along with whatever the mother says and does. His behavior passively supports the mother's correcting and nudging.

As the son gets older, the mother has even greater expectations. No matter how hard the son tries to succeed or to do it right, he never quite pleases her. His failure to do it right occurs, not because he's in a power struggle with his mother, but because he's a child with a child's ability. His parents respond to his mistakes, however, as if he were purposefully making mistakes to "get" them.

To protect himself from the constant criticism of "It's not good enough" and "Do it again," the child begins to set his *own* standards of behavior while simultaneously rejecting those of his parents. This maneuver is protective because it at least gives him a chance of pleasing someone—himself. It is also an angry response because he rejects the standards that those around him operate from.

The more the son operates from his own standards, the more frustrated his parents become. Their frustration gets translated into negative strokes to the child. Eventually the child comes to expect and be comfortable with this type of stroking. Also, because this child is not capable of walking away from his parents' anger, nor of taking them on directly, he goes underground with his anger. He "forgets," he dawdles, he doesn't finish jobs, he says he'll do something and then doesn't. No matter how hard he is pushed, he resists. The die is cast. The Caretaker mother is bound and determined to improve this child. The Passive Taker father idly watches. The child becomes Passive Aggressive.

If this family has a second child, that child will probably become a Caretaker because the parents now need someone who will cooperate, particularly since the mother already has her hands full with the Passive Taker father and the Passive Aggressive son. As with their first child, the parents expect a lot of the second, but they are not as critical with him since "he's only a child." In addition, the second child sees what's happening with his older brother, and he decides to follow a different path. In order to be recognized, he does things "right." Subconsciously, he does it right to compete with his sibling, who is doing it wrong. Also, the more he accomplishes, the more responsibility he is given, and the more he accomplishes. The die is cast.

In another family if the mother splits her time between the Caretaker and the Corrector positions, and the father is Passive Aggressive, the first-born most likely will become Caretaker/Corrector if a girl, and Passive Aggressive if a boy. The second child, regardless of sex, is likely to be scripted to be Passive Taker, since this position is the least demanding. If the mother and father have scripts that require a tyrant, both children will become Passive Aggressive because Passive Aggressives are the most difficult children to deal with and require the most energy.

Sometimes parents are simply too tired to raise yet another child. If these parents have a male child, this child will probably become Passive Aggressive, for he is allowed to determine what he wants to do and when he wants to do it. He will set his own standards of behavior. If the child is female, there is a good likelihood that she will become a Caretaker and take care of her parents. The child who is labeled "genius" usually becomes Passive Aggressive because he is thought of as special and often is allowed to do as he pleases.

A good deal of literature and data show that the first child is usually the high achiever in the family, whereas the second child tends to be less of an achiever. Yet we all can cite many families where this is not the case. In my clinical experience it seems that these first-born high achievers do not have Caretaker mothers who would score eight or more on the Caretaker Test or Passive Taker fathers who would score eight or higher.

Since my theory of position scripting is in its infancy, however, it will require more study and input from other clinicians in the field.

Who Marries Whom

Once you've lived some eighteen or more years of your life in a particular position, and it's time to choose a mate, your script position plays a large part in determining your selection.

Usually a person whose primary position is that of Caretaker will marry a person who is a Passive Taker or a Passive Aggressive. In this way the person can continue her life plan and caretake.

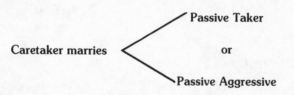

The Passive Taker most likely will select a Caretaker or a Corrector as a mate. Either selection allows this person to remain undirected and be told what to do.

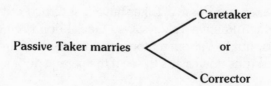

Corrector is likely to select a Passive Aggressive mate as a first choice, because this offers him a great excuse to be critical. Corrector's second choice is Passive Taker.

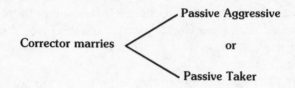

A Passive Aggressive person is likely to select a Corrector as a first choice, because a Corrector is more likely to help the Passive Aggressive reexperience the constant badgering and angry feelings directed toward him as a child. Passive Aggressive's second choice is that of Caretaker. Note that both these selections fulfill the Passive Aggressive's need to be pushed and nudged while he remains resistant.

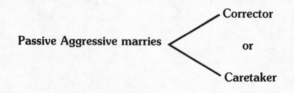

The Interrelationship of Positions

The following are everyday interactions of spouses in their various positions. You'll undoubtedly recognize yourself in a few of these situations.

—Caretaker and Passive Taker are sitting at the kitchen table having lunch. Passive Taker says, "Do we have any butter?" At which point Caretaker bounces up, runs to the refrigerator, and brings back the butter.

—Caretaker and Passive Taker have just turned out the lights to go to sleep when Passive Taker says, "Gee, I don't remember if the garage door is shut." Without a moment's hesitation, Caretaker jumps out of bed and runs downstairs to see if the garage door is shut. When

Caretaker gets back into bed, Passive Taker says, "You know, I don't remember if I let the dog out." Again Caretaker jumps up, runs downstairs, and lets the dog out. When Caretaker gets back into bed, Passive Taker says, "I wonder if the basement door is closed." Caretaker now moves to Angry Righteous and responds, "Darn you, I'm not about to get out of this bed again," and refuses to talk to her husband until the next morning.

—Passive Taker, standing in front of the refrigerator with his arms folded, says, "I can't find the jelly." Caretaker, sitting at the table, immediately gets up, goes to the refrigerator, moves the mayonnaise and pickle jars, and hands Passive Taker the jelly.

—Corrector expects Passive Aggressive husband to be on time for bridge club. He, as usual, runs fifteen to twenty minutes late.

—Caretaker and Corrector are taking a drive, when Corrector says, "Just listen to all these squeaks and rattles." Caretaker instantly feels anxious. As soon as they get home, she gets on the telephone and makes an appointment to have the car tuned.

—Corrector enjoys a neat house and is forever tidying up. Passive Aggressive leaves her nylons, makeup, curling iron, hair drier, and deodorant strewn about on the bathroom counter.

—Corrector hates smoking. When Corrector says something about a new finding that cigarettes cause brain damage, Passive Aggressive turns Rebellious and smokes even more.

—Corrector believes you should keep the gas tank at least half full. Passive Taker never thinks to look at the gas gauge and runs out of gas.

—Caretaker decides it would be nice to have sex tonight. In preparation, she buys some nice baby lotion in order to give her husband a massage to start the evening off. She prepares his favorite dinner, including coconut cream pie. After dinner she showers, puts on her best perfume, and slips into a sexy lounging outfit.

—Passive Taker thinks it would be nice to have sex tonight. He goes to bed and lies there.

—Corrector decides that it would be nice to have sex tonight. But he warns his spouse beforehand that his back has been hurting, so they'll have to be careful, and they'll have to go to bed early so he's not too tired in the morning, and he would appreciate it if she wouldn't wear that smelly dusting powder.

—Passive Aggressive also thinks it would be nice to have sex tonight. He calls his wife from the office and makes a proposal. That night, as his wife is preparing for bed thinking of the upcoming event, Passive Aggressive falls asleep in front of the television set.

—Caretaker plans a big party, and on the day of the big bash, some friends arrive to help. Caretaker has made lists for everyone, outlining what they are to do. Passive Aggressive goes to the store and forgets some of the items on his list. As Corrector sets up the bar, he comments, "People don't enjoy themselves at big parties, and besides, they usually drink too much." Passive Taker sits there and expects someone to read him his list because he forgot his glasses, except that he doesn't think to ask anyone to read him the list. Caretaker cuts up the vegetables, runs the vacuum cleaner, arranges the flowers, and stops and fixes lunch for the whole crew.

MOVING OUT OF YOUR SCRIPT POSITION

The problem with all these positions is that they limit how a person thinks and behaves. Also, when in one of these positions a person is unable to simultaneously take into account both himself and others. The Caretaker always focuses on others, discounts herself, and eventually feels resentful because her needs and wants are not recognized. The Passive Taker does not focus on himself or others but instead is a reactor to life; he never figures out what he wants or what others around him want. The Corrector focuses on the flaws and mistakes; he constantly browbeats himself, as well as his spouse, which makes both of their lives unpleasant. The Passive Aggressive focuses on himself and operates from his own standards; this translates into discounting his spouse and not living up to what he is capable of achieving.

Because it is so important for your marriage and for you to move beyond the limitations of these positions, here are some suggestions for change.

Beyond Caretaker

If you are a Caretaker, first realize and understand that a lot of your caretaking is done because you are following your script. Also, you caretake because you are dependent, so to speak, on those strokes others give you and those you give yourself for what you accomplish.

The big problem with the Caretaker position is that it puts all the responsibility on you for making everything work in the relationship, while it simultaneously discounts your spouse and his ability to take charge and do more. This position is also a setup for you to become a nag since day after day you meet others' needs while your own needs are discounted. It also creates incredible tension in the relationship. You feel anxious and overworked most of the time, and your husband feels guilty—not guilty enough to help equalize the relationship, but guilty enough to want to get away.

For example, if every time you gave a present to a friend she gave you nine presents back, it wouldn't take long before you would pull away from her. The reason is that you couldn't keep up with her—nor would you necessarily want to keep up with the number of presents she gave you. The same holds true for your spouse. He probably enjoys doing nice things for you and taking care of you some of the time, but he's not as driven as you are because he doesn't have your script messages. All that caretaking you do actually causes him to pull away from you.

This is perhaps one of the hardest things for a Caretaker to understand. As a Caretaker child, you were praised and loved for all you did. Now you think that if you do more, you will be loved and your marriage will be better. But doing more is counterproductive. You must do *less* instead of doing more to make your marriage better.

To move out of the Caretaker position, start by writing down those things that you do in the relationship versus all the things your husband does. Then work to balance out the list. If you both work the same amount of hours outside the home, your task will be easy: All you need to do is split everything that has to be done. If you're worried about certain things not getting done, like the plants not being watered or the birdcage not being cleaned because your husband is Passive Aggressive and plays I'll-Do-It-When-I-Get-Damn-Good-and-Ready, put those items on your half of the list. But keep the list as equal as possible. No marriage is fifty-fifty, but most good ones aim at that fifty-fifty mark.

If you don't have a job outside the home, you can still calculate your hours against his hours. Split the rest of the chores down the middle. I think it's a good idea to bring your spouse into this plan and try to negotiate who will do what. Many husbands are willing to go along with the idea—they just aren't going to initiate it.

I know this assignment sounds terribly radical, especially at first, if you are a die-hard Caretaker. At the same time, all those hours of caretaking have not gotten you a better marriage. So try this plan for six months and see for yourself the positive impact it will have on both you and your marriage. It does work! I guarantee it.

If your husband thinks you're crazy coming up with such a notion, decide anyway what you will give up doing. Perhaps you'll give up three chores a month. Then bite the bullet and give them up no matter how anxious it makes you feel or how many comments he makes to get you back in line. As you change and accept your change, he'll change, and your marriage will get better.

One woman I know tried to move out of the Caretaker position a number of times before she was successful. It wasn't only her script and her husband who wanted her in this position, but her children also had an investment in it. After a rather light meal, one son said, "Mom, you never cook anymore." She still cooked plenty, about fourteen meals a week for various people, but certainly not on the grand scale her family was accustomed to. Then another son complained that all she seemed to do recently was tell others what to do. This comment came in response to her deciding that she wasn't going to do any of the dishes after a big turkey dinner she had prepared and served alone. So be aware, for even children will try to keep you in the Caretaker position.

Second, think of some things that *you* enjoy doing. For example, do you like to go to the movies, read, knit, take long soaks in the bathtub, or play racquetball? Once you decide what you enjoy, make a decision that each day you will do something for yourself. I know that if your spouse asked you to do one thing for him each day, you would have no trouble fitting it into your busy schedule. Therefore, you can do one nice thing for yourself. This will help to replace some of the strokes you'll be giving up because you'll no longer be doing as much for others.

One other thing to keep in mind: As you move out of the Caretaker position, you will experience a terrible sense of loneliness. This is because you don't know what to do with your time if you're not caretaking. And this is one of the biggest reasons why Caretakers keep making pacts with themselves to do less in their marriage, then go back and do more. Only if you accept the pain of loneliness that always accompanies giving up the Caretaker position will you be able to move beyond this position and become your own person. Also, remember that you'll still be a caring person and you'll still do nice things for your spouse. Now, however, these things will be based on a decision in which you've taken into account *both* yourself and your spouse.

Beyond Passive Taker

If you are a Passive Taker, your job is to get involved in life and live it to the fullest, which is ultimately going to be fun. You can start by deciding to plan one thing each week that you and your wife would enjoy, such as going to a movie, going to the botanical gardens, or shopping for antiques.

Also, keep a written log of everything your spouse does for you. Keeping this log is in itself a way to get out of the Passive Taker position because it helps you focus on what's going on around you. Then, for everything your wife has done for you, do twice as much back for her. Your accounting might look like this:

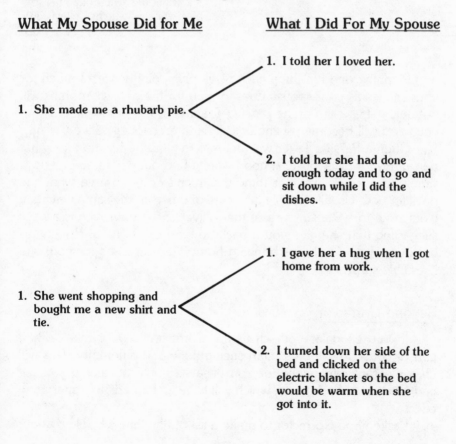

What My Spouse Did for Me　　　**What I Did For My Spouse**

1. I told her I loved her.

1. She made me a rhubarb pie.

2. I told her she had done enough today and to go and sit down while I did the dishes.

1. I gave her a hug when I got home from work.

1. She went shopping and bought me a new shirt and tie.

2. I turned down her side of the bed and clicked on the electric blanket so the bed would be warm when she got into it.

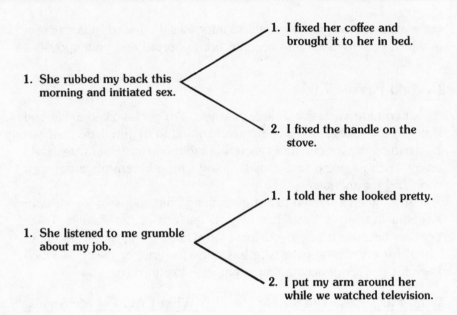

1. She rubbed my back this morning and initiated sex.

    1. I fixed her coffee and brought it to her in bed.

    2. I fixed the handle on the stove.

1. She listened to me grumble about my job.

    1. I told her she looked pretty.

    2. I put my arm around her while we watched television.

Planning one fun thing each week plus doing twice as much for your spouse as your spouse does for you for the next six months will not only get you out of the Passive Taker position, but it will energize you. You will become psychologically and emotionally alive.

Often a Passive Taker will moan to me that he has no idea what he can do for his spouse. A good way to find out what you can do is simply to ask her. Another thing you might do is observe what she does for you. Usually people take care of others in the same way they would like to be taken care of themselves. So if your wife is always suggesting that she give you a backrub, you can bet that she enjoys backrubs. If she's always bringing home little surprises for you, she likes little surprises.

Beyond Corrector

If you recognize yourself as the Corrector in your relationship, part of your job will be to start seeing the world differently. This will be a pleasant experience for you because you'll be seeing yourself and others more positively, which will have an immediately energizing effect.

I asked one Corrector to make a list of fifty things he liked about himself. Like others, he expressed dismay at my asking for fifty items, but he did come up with them. Then each morning at breakfast he would read over his list. In three months he found himself automatically focusing on things he liked about himself and other people around him. The change was wonderful not only for him, but for his family as well.

Another technique to help you move out of the Corrector position is to write down fifteen things each day that you enjoy. This again helps you focus on the positive things in life. Here's a list one woman made:

—It makes me happy to hear my husband singing in the shower.
—Today I looked at and enjoyed the architecture in my neighborhood.
—I felt good seeing all the fall flowers on my way to work.
—I enjoyed the hug and kiss my daughter gave me before I dropped her off at school.
—I enjoyed smelling my perfume during the day.
—I found a new herb tea I enjoyed.
—One of the other teachers at school told me my hair looked nice.
—A student I had last year gave me a big smile when I passed her in the corridor.
—I enjoyed hearing the sound of the dry leaves under my feet.
—I liked the feeling I got when I left school and went outside in the chilly air.
—I like the feel of my new coat.
—I'm happy that my new car is an automatic.
—I had a letter from a friend when I got home.
—I enjoyed watching my girls play in the bathtub this evening.

A third technique for getting out of the Corrector position is to give your spouse two compliments every single day. This will also help you change your focus.

Beyond Passive Aggressive

If you're Passive Aggressive, you have a lot of work ahead of you and it's not going to be easy because you'll have to start forcing yourself to adapt to the standards that other people follow. But you can do it.

One of the first things you might do is write down the things that seem to make your mate angry. Decide which of these behaviors you would be willing to change. If you're always running late and your mate always gets angry about your being late, make a pact with yourself to be on time. If she's irritated with you for not picking up your clothes, make a pact with yourself to pick up your clothes. If she frequently complains about your reckless driving, change the way you behave behind the wheel.

Try to come up with five behaviors that you will change over the next month, and then monitor your behavior. Most Passive Aggressives I have worked with are very bright people, and once they set their minds to something, they can accomplish it.

Second, no more temper tantrums. Many techniques are available for learning to control your anger. The one that seems to be most effective with the people I've worked with in therapy is saying two or three thousand times a day, "Nobody needs to get that angry." When I first present this idea, people look at me like I'm a little nuts; how can anyone say something two or three thousand times a day? Actually, you can say this phrase about forty times a minute. This exercise takes less than an hour and a half, and you can do it while you're showering, blow-drying your hair, commuting, cleaning out the dishwasher, or sitting in the dentist's office. Just say the phrase on and off and over and over throughout the day when you have mental downtime.

I'm sure there's always a first, but I've never had anyone who couldn't control his anger after he started using this method. The way it works is that when you become angry, this phrase automatically comes into your head, which helps you see that you do have a choice and you can stay in control. If this specific phrase doesn't quite strike you, make up one that has more meaning for you. One woman used the phrase "I don't need to scream and yell to get my point across."

Most people who use this technique find it helpful after three or four weeks. If you have been having angry explosions for a good part of your life, however, I suggest you use this method for three months or more.

Another technique for getting your anger under control is to put a large X on your calendar every time you have a major temper tantrum. Give yourself a small x for minor blowups. This exercise works because it keeps forcing you to reckon with the information of just how much you do lose your temper.

Third, because you have been operating from the "I-count-more-than-you-count" position for many years, you'll want to shift your emphasis somewhat and start doing things to show your mate that he or she also counts. You can do this easily by doing one or two nice things for your spouse each day that she would like you to.

One Passive Aggressive fellow carried around a little notebook wherever he went. He used the notebook to monitor his behavior continually. If anyone got angry at him, he wrote it down; later he examined what he had done that was provocative. If he had a tantrum, he wrote it down; then he reviewed his behavior and looked at what he could have done differently in the situation. He also recorded all the nice things he had done for his wife each day, which constantly called to his attention how much he was or wasn't doing.

It took this man about a year and a half, with many slips in between, but today he would not score more than two or three on the Passive Aggressive Test. In addition, he likes himself a whole lot more, his wife likes him a whole lot more, and he is no longer modeling Passive Aggressive behaviors for his children.

Energy, Energy

All of these techniques take work. And most people expect their marriage to change immediately. But it doesn't happen that way. It takes time and energy and more energy to turn a relationship around. At the same time, spending six months, a year, or even a year and a half working on yourself and making your marriage better is nothing compared to the pain that comes with a bad relationship. So put in the energy and make your marriage a loving one.

Giving Your Spouse an Assist

Even though your primary job is to change yourself, you might want to help your spouse change as well. If your spouse is a Caretaker, the best way to help her out of this position is to insist on doing more things yourself in the marriage. Also, encourage her to take better care of herself. Ask her to go on a walk with you; buy her a bicycle; give her a membership to a gym. And give her a lot of praise for just being *her*. In addition, stay in touch with ways you might subconsciously be encouraging her to stay in the Caretaker position.

If your spouse is a Passive Taker, stop rescuing him by making all the decisions. If you ask him what he wants to drink and he says, "You decide," you can say, "No, you decide." If you say it playfully, he'll get the point and won't think you're being sarcastic. But don't pour anything until he declares himself, for if you decide for him, you're not doing him or yourself a favor. Also, push him to do more things with you. Invite him to go shopping; get involved in a project together. If you're sitting and talking and he's sitting like a bump on a log, stop, get up, go over to him, sit on his lap, and say, "Your turn to talk."

When I work with Passive Takers, I'm always bombarding them with Nerf balls and telling them I'm going to have to get out my bellows and pump some life into them. They laugh and they do change, but it takes a lot of kidding and playful nudging to get them to come around and be a participant instead of an observer of life.

If your mate is a Corrector, simply point out her Corrector comments but do it matter-of-factly as opposed to angrily. When she takes a potshot at you by asking a question with a hidden agenda, such as, "You're going back to that same tailor you used last time?" you can say, "Sounds like you don't like the tailor I used last time." And when she makes a negative statement such as, "You're sure starting to get poochy," you can say, "Ugh," and hold your stomach, indicating you feel wounded. Or you can say, "That's two," indicating that she has now made two critical comments. Often when I suggest this tactic, people are aghast and tell me, "Oh, she'd be furious." If you say it playfully, however, people usually don't get angry. And if you find your spouse does get mad when you use this technique, then don't use it. No sense setting up either of you. Also, you can ask your mate what you might do to make her aware of her critical remarks, because most Correctors are oblivious to their own criticism. Remember, you can use any number of techniques. Choose the one that works best in your marriage.

If your spouse is Passive Aggressive, you must decide to stop getting so angry at him or her. This is incredibly difficult because Passive Aggressives have a way of intruding in your life. For example, they use the last piece of toilet paper on the roll and there you are. They tell you they will pick up the children from soccer practice at 6:30, and they don't get to the field until 7:15. Remember, each time you respond to their behavior with too much anger, you inadvertently reinforce their position because they once again get the negative strokes so familiar to them. Also, your anger gives them ammunition to fight back. And if you get too angry, they can focus on your anger and don't have to look at their own behavior. Or they can justify their own temper tantrum in response to yours.

You also must not ignore their bad behavior; if you do, you are covertly supporting their Passive Aggressive position. Instead, you must respond in a middle-of-the-road fashion, which is darn difficult. For example, you might say to the toilet paper offender, "The next time you use the last piece of toilet tissue, I would appreciate it if you would put on a new roll." To the spouse who has failed to pick up the children at 6:30, you might say, "When you find you're running late, call and I'll get the children or try to make other arrangements."

Also, expect that it will take a good year to a year and a half before your spouse gets out of this position. It'll be worth the work and the wait, however.

It's a Matter of Choice

No one would consciously choose any of these script positions in marriage, because they do not help people live up to their full potential. Nevertheless, you're more than likely caught in one of these positions, and it's going to take a lot of effort to change. And even as you work at it, you'll start to slip back at times since your script messages and games support this position. Also, everyone you know has come to expect this particular behavior from you, and to behave differently will feel unnatural both to you and to them.

But you *can* change. And on looking back, you'll see that the energy you put out was well worth it since there are few things in life that are more meaningful or satisfying than a good relationship.

10

CONTROL- AND ATTENTION- COMPETITIVE

WHO RUNS THE SHOW AND WHO GETS TAKEN CARE OF

One thing I continually point out in marriage counseling is that when a couple has a disagreement, often they are not fighting about the issue they think they are. Instead, they are disagreeing about who's going to be in control of the relationship or who's going to get the attention in the relationship.[1] For inadvertently most people compete with their spouse for control or for attention. And some spouses go so far as to compete both for control and for attention. In fact, almost every disagreement that a couple has includes the underlying issue of who will control the relationship, or who will get the attention in the relationship. In therapy, when someone is competing for control, I tell him he's being Control-Competitive.* If I see that he is competing for attention, I tell him he's being Attention-Competitive.* I coined these phrases some years ago to help people understand what's really going on when they have an argument.

Control-Competitive

At my dad's sixty-third birthday party, my husband and I were talking with another couple we barely knew. The wife was telling us how they were going to miss their eighteen-year-old son, who was going off to college in the fall. Not only were they going to miss him, but they were going to miss his working around the house.

The husband said his son had cut the grass for the past six years, and he wasn't particularly looking forward to taking over that job again. The wife agreed that it was really going to be tough to get all the grass cut each week. So naturally, I asked her how much grass they had to cut.

The wife said, "About two acres." The husband said, "No, dear, it's not quite that much." She turned to him and said, "Why, it's every bit that much!" At that point the husband reached out and put his hand on his wife's knee. (If he could have gotten by with it, he probably would have put his hand across her mouth.) Then he said emphatically, "It's not two acres, *dear*." (Notice how couples often call each other "dear" when they're angry.)

I said their discussion reminded me of one my husband and I had had the day before. A friend who was visiting asked me how big our refrigerator was. I said I thought it was about nineteen cubic feet. My husband looked at me and said, "No, *dear*, it's only seventeen cubic feet." I instantly felt the urge to strangle him. But because my mother taught me that polite people don't argue in public, I simply glared at him. Not too long after the discussion about the size of our refrigerator, our friend had to leave. Thank goodness, because I couldn't wait to tell my husband he was wrong about the size of our refrigerator. As I shut the front door behind our friend, I turned to my husband and said indignantly, "The refrigerator is nineteen cubic feet. And stop disagreeing with me in public! And don't call me 'dear' when you disagree with me!!"

Exchanges such as this go on all the time in relationships. The husband says, "It took us about four hours to get to Chicago." And before he has the words out of his mouth, the wife is saying, "I think it took more like five." He says, "No, *darling*, don't you remember? We left at four but had to stop at the drugstore and the post office, and those stops ate up some time." To which she counters, "But, *darling*, even taking those stops into account, it still took us over five hours to drive to Chicago." Now the couple is arguing about how long it took to get to Chicago, and they have forgotten that they were talking to someone else.

When a couple becomes embroiled in such a fight, they think what they are fighting over are the facts. I've seen couples run for the encyclopedia and the road atlas to prove whose point was right. One couple went so far as to tape-record a fight they were having, and bring me the tape so I could listen to it and judge who was right. I said, "No way, I'm not going to play judge and jury." Besides, the real issue was not who was right, but who was going to be in control in the relationship.

What difference does it make to the story if it takes four hours or five hours to drive to Chicago, unless you're going to drive there? And what difference does it make how many cubic feet a refrigerator happens to have, unless you're in the market for a refrigerator? It makes a big difference, however, to the couple embroiled in the argument, because they are Control-Competitive. What they're really fighting over is who's going to be in control in the relationship—who's going to run the show and who's going to have the last word. To each of them, it seems as though they are fighting for their survival. And in some sense, they are. Each person is fighting for the position that he or she has grown up with, which is the position of being in control and calling the shots. This accounts for the intense feelings each of them experiences during the disagreement. The people who are most likely to be Control-Competitive are Caretakers, Correctors, and Passive Aggressives, because all these people like to control the situation and have their own way.

In many areas of their life, the couple who is Control-Competitive has defined either verbally or nonverbally who's in charge. He may handle the finances while she handles the disciplining of the children. He feeds the dog and she folds the laundry. If they grocery-shop together, she gets the check cashed and directs which aisles they go down, while he pushes the cart. When they take a trip, she does the driving, and he plays navigator.

The problem comes when no precedent has been set for doing a particular task. For example, my husband and I are Control-Competitive, and one of our worst fights was over who was going to be in charge of the houseplants. The fight took place in the fall, when it was time to move our plants indoors. Some of the plants were too large for me to move by myself, so I asked my husband to help. Within

five minutes I felt that he was no longer helping me but rather direct-
ing me.

The first offensive comment I remember him making was, "Why
are you keeping this straggly plant?" (Note the hidden agenda.) Then
he handed me another plant and said, "You take this one to the family
room." When I returned and found him pruning one of my favorite
plants, I was outraged. I recall thinking, "How dare he! I'm the one
who takes care of the plants. I water them; I feed them; I repot them.
And I decide if they need to be pitched or cut back. These plants are
my territory." I also remember shouting something like, "Everytime
we work together, you have to be in charge."

Looking back, it's easy to see what was happening in this situation.
We both are used to taking charge and being in control. We are very
goal-oriented, get-the-job-done, be-in-charge persons. In our careers
these traits work well for us. On the homefront they usually work well.
Through the years, we have established our own areas of being in
charge. I usually decide what should be done to the inside of the
house, whereas he takes charge of the outside (except for my rose
garden). I also make most of the arrangements for our social life, and
he plans all our vacations. When we give a party, I do the planning
and preparation, and he helps. When the guests arrive, he takes the
coats and fixes the drinks. After the party, I put the food away and
put the dishes in the dishwasher, while he picks up the glasses and gets
the trash together. I wash the crystal; he dries it and puts it away. While
we're cleaning up, we laugh and talk and it's very nice; we have our
own areas of being in charge. Someone from the outside looking in on
us after a party might even say we work very well together. The reality,
however, is that we work well side-by-side. And there is a difference.

In those instances that call for an in-charge person and a helper,
such as when we hang wallpaper or rake leaves, I voluntarily move
to the helper position and my husband is the person in charge. I don't
have any competitive feelings about this arrangement, and I'm willing
to be the helper.

When it came to carrying in the houseplants that fall, however,
we were in trouble. He automatically moved to his familiar position
of being in charge, and I moved to my familiar position of being in
charge. And since I already was accustomed to being in charge of the
houseplants, I felt justified in my stance. He was going to be my helper,
and I was not going to be his.

As the years have passed, my husband and I have had fewer problems of this type, not because we have become less Control-Competitive, but because we each know who will be in charge of what area. When something new comes up, however, it's back to the same old Control-Competitive feelings.

I write a weekly newspaper column, and each week after I've finished, my husband edits it. After he's finished going over the material, we sit down together and he gives me his feedback, which is good because he often sees what I don't. What we fight over, however, is not his feedback, but who holds the pencil. Who has the pencil signifies who has the control. Generally I can laugh at this because I know what's going on, but sometimes I reach over and take the pencil from his hand.

One couple I have been working with readily admit they're Control-Competitive. They've had some real battles, such as the one they had about where to put the remote control for the electric garage-door opener when it's not in use. The husband wanted to keep it in the glove box so no one would see it or get any funny ideas about stealing it. The wife thought that wasn't practical, however, because to get to the opener she had to stop the car, unlock her seat belt, scoot over on the seat, and search for it in the glove box. Consequently, she wanted it clipped onto the sun visor. When she drove the car, she would get the garage-door opener out of the glove box and clip it to the visor. When he drove the car, he would put it back in the glove box.

They also had a Control-Competitive issue over decorating the house. When they hung pictures, he wanted them all hung in a straight line over the sofa. She, on the other hand, thought they looked better in a random arrangement.

This couple also disagreed over what things to set out on their coffee table. She wanted a candy dish, antique candlesticks, and an ashtray. In addition to these items, he wanted a few art books and his paperweight collection on the table. He enjoyed having many things on display, whereas she thought it looked better to have only a few things on the table.

In the end, even they had a good laugh over the situation they now refer to as the Coffee Table Incident. One evening when they were expecting guests, the wife went into the living room, filled the candy dish, and did a last-minute check to make sure everything was in order. She then went into the kitchen to make final preparations.

While she was in the kitchen, her husband sneaked into the living room and quietly put out the art books and his paperweights. When the guests arrived and everyone gathered in the living room, the wife saw the coffee table. "I couldn't believe it," she told me later. "When I caught my husband's eye, he winked at me." At that moment she was able to see how this was another Control-Competitive issue. She grinned and winked back and decided then and there that she was no longer going to fight over control of the coffee table. He could put out what he wanted.

• Typical Control-Competitive Behaviors

The following are examples of common Control-Competitive behaviors between husbands and wives:

—The wife researches the various coffee makers on the market and then asks for a certain one for her birthday. The husband buys her a different kind of coffee maker that he has read about and thinks is better. The husband is being Control-Competitive.

—A friend asks the husband what book he would recommend for someone starting to play bridge. The husband recommends one, and his wife comments, "That's not the book to start with. Try so-and-so instead." Both spouses are equally talented bridge players. This wife is being Control-Competitive.

—The wife tells a story about someone at a party and mentions that her hair was dyed a greenish blue. To which the Control-Competitive husband responds, "Oh, no, it was more a bluish green."

—The husband is telling his friend that he and his wife didn't get home last night from the party until 2:30 a.m. The wife butts in and says, "It was more like a quarter to three." The wife is being Control-Competitive.

• What to Do If You and Your Spouse Are Control-Competitive

If you and your spouse are Control-Competitive, define as much as possible who runs *what* show.

For example, a couple can decide in advance that when they garden, he will be her helper, and when they wallpaper, she will be his. Or she will decide how the towels should be hung in the bathroom, and he will decide what route to take going to his mother's house. It's not appropriate, however, to decide what decisions your spouse can make; if you do this, you are being Control-Competitive and still trying to run the show. That's why, when you do a trade-off, it's better to say, "I would like to make this decision. What decision do you want to make?"

In all those other areas where you can't possibly anticipate that a power struggle is in the offing, establish some ground rules for yourselves before a disagreement arises. For example, make a pact that you will not correct each other in public. And if your mate says, "It's 972 miles to New York," and you think it's really only 950, you will be quiet even if you *know* your mate is wrong.

You also can decide to use the statement "Let's just agree to disagree" when you find yourself caught in one of these power struggles. One couple told me that they had tried this suggestion and it didn't work at all. When either one of them said, "Let's agree to disagree," the other would say, "I'm not ready to stop this discussion yet!"

I suggested to them that if he was able to show enough restraint and call the battle to a halt, surely she could show enough restraint and agree to disagree. And if she was able to say, "Let's agree to disagree," he could show the same restraint and stop the fight. They agreed with the premise, and since then many of their Control-Competitive arguments have stopped.

Attention-Competitive

Just as couples compete for who's going to be in control, couples also compete for who's going to get taken care of in the relationship. When this competition is going on, the couple is Attention-Competitive. Passive Takers and Passive Aggressives are most likely to be Attention-Competitive because they both expect to be taken care of.

One of my favorite examples of being Attention-Competitive comes from a couple I was working with in counseling. The husband would come home at night, step inside the door, and yell, "Hello?" This "Hello?" (spoken as a question) announced to the family that Dad was home and that everyone should come greet Dad and give him attention.

The wife felt irritated at this greeting because she, too, wanted to get some attention and be taken care of when her husband came home. After all, she had been struggling with three children during the day. She also thought that at least some of the time her husband should come find her and say, "Hello" (not as a question), thus recognizing her.

This fellow used another Attention-Competitive maneuver when his wife made a request of him. She would say, "Let's go to the patio and talk," and he would say, "If you really want me to." Well, of course she wanted him to, or she wouldn't have suggested it. His comment, however, was a way of inviting his wife to back down from what she wanted, and to give him what he wanted, which was not to go to the patio and talk.

Unfortunately, because her script called for her not to be taken care of in life (her mother had died when she was a child and her father was an alcoholic), she would back down and say to her husband, "It's okay, we can talk later. Why don't you do what you want to do now." Clearly she was the Caretaker in their relationship.

We all have heard or participated in these exchanges. For example, one spouse says, "What a lousy day I've had," and the partner responds with, "It couldn't have been as lousy as mine." Or one mate says what a terrific job he did, and his mate counters with what an extra-terrific job she did. Here the competition is over who should be most applauded and recognized, another form of getting taken care of.

In addition to competing directly for who's going to get taken care of in the relationship, a person often will manipulate his mate by making vague statements that invite his partner to do something for him. Such comments as "Gee, it would sure be nice to have some popcorn," "A cold beer would sure taste good about now," or "I wonder what time it's getting to be," are requests to get taken care of. However, the spouse making the request does not "own," or take responsibility for, what he wants. If his wife gets up and makes popcorn, gets him a beer, or finds out the time for him, at some later point she may feel entitled to make a request of him. But because he doesn't recognize even to himself what his wife has done for him, he doesn't think about taking care of her in return.

What this situation calls for is a direct statement by the wife, such as, "Sounds as though you'd like me to make you some popcorn." Then it becomes the responsibility of her husband to own that he is asking her to take care of him.

Another subtle way to be Attention-Competitive is to invite your spouse to make a decision for you that is *your* decision to make. For example, a wife asks her husband, "Would you like iced tea or coffee with your dinner, honey?" and Passive Taker honey answers, "Whatever." Now it falls to the wife to take responsibility and decide what he wants to drink.

Another classic Attention-Competitive response is "I don't know." The wife asks her husband if he wants to go to the movies tonight, and he says, "I don't know." This immediately puts her in the position of taking responsibility and making the decision, even if that decision is simply to drop the idea.

Many times in conversation a spouse will start talking about a particular issue, and instead of her mate making a comment about what she is saying, or even asking a question that encourages her to go on talking, he'll say nothing. And soon she starts to "feel" that her husband is not interested. So she'll switch the conversation to him and ask him about his day.

Or, she'll be telling him something about her day and he'll get a telephone call. After he finishes his telephone conversation, he starts talking about something that interests him, and he fails to refocus the conversation back on her and what she was talking about. He simply does not attune himself to what she is interested in.

A lot of women complain to me that their husbands don't take care of them. And yet they tell me they get flowers and nice presents, and taken out to lunch, and they have lovely homes and good sex lives. So why don't they *feel* taken care of?

The wife doesn't feel taken care of because in almost all of her interactions with her husband, he doesn't focus on her but subconsciously sets it up for the focus of attention to be on him. This causes the wife to feel not taken care of. And she isn't being taken care of emotionally, because she is rarely the center of attention. Instead the husband is usually the center of attention. He is Attention-Competitive.

People are Attention-Competitive in a relationship not because they don't get taken care of enough, but because as children they got the lion's share of the attention in the family and that's what feels most natural to them as adults. Spouses who are Attention-Competitive actually get taken care of far more than their mates, because they know and subconsciously work all the angles.

● Typical Attention-Competitive Behaviors

The following are examples of common Attention-Competitive behaviors that often occur between spouses:

—The wife gets sick, and her husband gets angry and pouts because she's sick and doesn't make him dinner. He expects to be taken care of. This husband is clearly Attention-Competitive.

—The wife goes on a job interview. That evening when she comes home the husband fails to bring up the interview. Instead he talks about his day at the office. The husband is Attention-Competitive.

—Husband and wife are walking around in the department store, and neither of them thinks about where they're going. Neither of them is willing to take charge; both are competing for who gets taken care of.

—The wife is lying in bed with the flu. The two-year-old is running around the house with dirty diapers. The four-year-old keeps coming in and telling Mommy he's hungry. The husband comes into the bedroom, looks at his wife, and says, "What do you want me to do?" Instead of picking up the ball and making the decision himself regarding what needs to be done, this husband invites his wife to take care of him by asking her to direct the situation. Clearly this husband is Attention-Competitive.

—Husband and wife are standing in the family room when their teenage daughter walks in limping. The husband looks at his wife and says, "What's wrong with her foot?" Instead of taking care of his daughter and asking her directly what's wrong, the husband is competing for attention with both his daughter and his wife by asking his wife to explain the situation and thereby focus on him.

—The wife is home preparing dinner and expects her husband to arrive any minute. The phone rings, and when she answers, he says, "Hi?" The "Hi?" (with a question mark) translates into, "I hope you're not going to be angry with me for being late, but rather you'll take care of me by reassuring me that I'm not going to be in the doghouse." Instead of taking care of his wife and apologizing because he is late, the husband tries to finagle his wife into taking care of him. He is Attention-Competitive.

—Husband and wife go shopping together, and she browses in the shoe store for a half hour, looking at the various shoe styles and asking his opinion. The husband then says he would like to go to the bookstore. Five minutes after they get to the bookstore, she is nudging him to hurry along. This Attention-Competitive wife only wants to do what *she* wants to do, and she expects her husband to take care of her.

—The husband who is retired and stays home all day says to his wife as she comes in from working all day, "What's for dinner?" This guy is clearly Attention-Competitive.

—The wife knows her husband has slept poorly the previous night. She says, "How did you sleep last night?" The wife is inviting her husband to reassure her that everything is okay. The wife is Attention-Competitive.

—Husband and wife are getting undressed, and he says, "Don't you want to make love to me?" This husband is being Attention-Competitive; instead of approaching her and saying by his actions that she's desirable, he expects his wife to reassure him that he's desirable.

● What to Do If You and Your Spouse Are Attention-Competitive

If you recognize that your mate is competing with you for who's going to get taken care of in the marriage, you have the option of saying, "Hey, wait a minute. It's my turn to be taken care of." This is what the woman who had the flu and the man who was browsing in the bookstore should have said.

If your mate makes no comments as you are talking and you start to feel anxious and emotionally abandoned, say something about his seeming lack of interest. Point out that he hasn't made any comments or asked any questions, which indicates that he is not being attentive to you.

If your spouse is angling for you to do him a favor without taking responsibility and asking directly, you can point out what he is doing with a statement of your own, such as, "It sounds as though you want me to get up and find out what time it's getting to be." Another way to handle this problem is to tell your spouse directly what you see happening. Most people find the information fascinating and helpful, and as they understand what they are doing, they can stop these Attention-Competitive maneuvers.

If the competition seems always to revolve around the same issue, decide how the two of you will handle it when it comes up in the future. Remember the fellow I saw in marriage counseling who said "Hello?" when he came in at night? He made an agreement to come in the house, say nothing, go find his wife, and give her a nice hug to announce that he was home. Being sought out allowed his wife to feel important and cared for, and the hug allowed them both to be taken care of. Also, his wife agreed that when this fellow used his famous line "If you really want me to" in response to a request from her, she would answer him by saying, "I really want you to."

Control/Attention-Competitive All in One Breath

Some transactions are simultaneously Control/Attention-Competitive.* In my experience the person who is most adept at this behavior is the spouse who operates from the Passive Aggressive, center-of-the-world position. So naturally this spouse competes to be in control and to get taken care of, all in one transaction.

A classic example of being Control/Attention-Competitive is the wife who goes around the house acting angry but, when her husband asks her what's wrong, says, "Nothing." The way she says "Nothing," of course, denotes that plenty is wrong and that her husband better not take what she says at face value. So again he says, "Come on, what's wrong?" and she enunciates carefully, "Nothing." Each time she says "Nothing," she's in control. And each time he asks her what's wrong, she gets her husband's attention.

If your spouse gives you the old "Nothing is wrong" routine, make a statement to her such as, "Your tone of voice and the way you're acting tell me something is wrong. When you're ready to talk about it, let me know, because I'd like to work it out."

Another example of this type of transaction is the spouse who doesn't give enough information when he's talking. He says something like, "Ron and I went out to lunch today and he was telling me . . . ," and his wife has absolutely no idea who Ron is. Or he says, "People were sure acting strange at work today," and then says nothing further. This forces his wife to ask for more of the details, which keeps him in control and also gets him attention as his wife is forced to focus on him and ask more questions.

If your mate doesn't give you enough information when he's talking, you can say, "You're not giving me enough information, which is a way to get my attention because I have to keep asking what you mean. So, tell me again, and this time give me all the information."

Talking too slowly, speaking too softly, talking on-and-on-and-on, and not completing sentences but leaving it up to one's mate to complete them are four additional Control/Attention-Competitive transactions that guarantee both control of the situation and attention for oneself.

If your spouse talks too slowly, push her to speed up. A statement such as, "Come on, Jane, talk faster," probably will do the trick. If he talks too softly, you can say, "Will you please talk louder?" If she talks on-and-on-and-on, you might say in a playful manner, "Come on, Mary, what's the bottom line?" And if he doesn't complete sentences, you can say, "You're not finishing your sentence." Or you can finish his sentence in a nonsensical and playful fashion, and the two of you can have a good laugh while still calling attention to the problem.

I use all these techniques in therapy, and they are quite effective in getting the person to see what he or she is doing.

A COMPETITIVE BEHAVIOR QUIZ

Although some competitive behaviors are hard to spot, others are fairly easy. The following questions will help you pinpoint which competitive behaviors you most frequently use in your marriage. Answer each question with a yes or no.

_____ Do you correct your mate in public?

_____ Do you often insist on having the last word?

_____ Do you usually insist on taking charge of a situation?

_____ Do you frequently correct or clarify what your mate has said?

_____ Are you often accused of mumbling or talking too softly by your mate?

_____ Do you frequently tell your mate nothing is wrong but act as if there _is_ something wrong?

_____ Do you tend to talk on . . . and on . . . and on without giving your spouse a chance to talk?

_____ Do you find that your mate often needs to ask you for more information when you are telling a story in order that he or she understands what you're talking about?

_____ Do you have a habit of beating around the bush when you want something instead of asking for what you want directly?

_____ Do you look to your spouse to make most of the decisions because you have difficulty making them?

_____ Do you often say, "Do you really want me to?" after your spouse has already said she wants you to?

_____ Do you ask your mate what she thinks, and then after she tells you, you explain to her that what she thinks is wrong?
_____ Do you introduce subjects for conversation that only you are interested in?
_____ Do you frequently change the topic of conversation from what your spouse is talking about to what you want to talk about?

Each question that you have answered with a *yes* points to the fact that you are competing with your spouse, either to run the show or to be taken care of.

Once you know your areas of weakness, make a pact with yourself to stop these competitive behaviors. And watch how dramatically your marriage improves. It's not magic . . . but almost.

THE
DRAMA
TRIANGLE

RUNNING AROUND THE DRAMA TRIANGLE

As you've been learning, you do all sorts of things that cause you problems in your marriage. Even when you know what you should be doing differently, you still don't always do it. Why? Because old habits are hard to break, and change takes a lot of work. And too, sometimes even after you have changed, you slip back into old nonproductive behaviors.

Not long ago I found myself back in the Caretaker position. I had mentioned to my husband that we needed to get a baby-sitter for Saturday night. He said, "I'll call Mom, or maybe I'll ask John what he's doing." To which I answered, "No, that's all right, I'll take care of it. I probably have more time this week than you do with your schedule." He said, "Fine." And I went to my note pad to write down my latest duty.

As I was looking over the list of things I had to do, I found myself thinking, "I'm never going to get everything done this week." And then I moved to, "And now I have to make arrangements for a baby-sitter. Why do I have to do everything around this house?"

Luckily for me and my husband, I caught myself and thought, "How ridiculous I'm being. Skeeter just offered to help me, and I turned him down. And now I'm angry because I have to make arrangements for the baby-sitter Saturday night."

One way to analyze what happened in this situation is by using the Drama Triangle.[1] There are three roles on the triangle: Rescuer, Victim, and Persecutor.

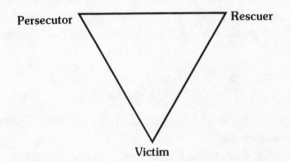

The Rescuer takes care of someone because he thinks he *should*. The Victim feels *helpless*, or is seen by others as *helpless*. And the Persecutor uses various forms of anger to strike out at others.

Regarding the baby-sitter situation, I got on the triangle as a Rescuer when I suggested that I get the sitter; I've been scripted to take care of people. When I looked over my list and thought, "I'm never going to get everything done this week," I started to feel overwhelmed. At that point I moved from a Rescuer to a Victim. Then, when I thought, "Why do I have to do everything around here?" I moved from the Victim to the Persecutor. Fortunately, I caught myself before I persecuted my husband verbally.

Unfortunately this kind of behavior often goes on in a marriage. One spouse will become the Rescuer, then feel like a Victim, and then move to Persecutor. Sometimes these switches from Rescuer to Victim to Persecutor take place only in one's head, as it happened with me. At other times they occur out loud. When the husband and the wife are involved in such an interchange, each of them may end up on the Drama Triangle. One spouse may take the Victim role while the other takes the Persecutor role, or one will be the Rescuer while the other spouse is the Victim.

People move from one role to another and fairly rapidly. Also, there is no set pattern to the way people rotate around the triangle. Most people have a tendency to keep getting on the triangle at the same place. If you are a Caretaker, your point of entry will usually be the Rescuer, since you take care of people. If you are a Passive Taker, you're likely to get on as a Victim, since you appear or feel helpless. If you are a Corrector, you'll probably start as a Persecutor, since your focus tends to be the other person's flaw. If you are Passive Aggressive, you're likely to get on the triangle anywhere, depending on how you feel at that particular moment. Despite where you get on, however, you'll soon find yourself in all three roles unless you choose to get off the triangle.

On the Triangle with Meat and Potatoes

Here's an example of how one couple got on the Drama Triangle after work one evening.

Mary comes home from work dead tired. She's not particularly hungry. She doesn't feel like cooking, and a sandwich would be just fine with her. But she knows that John is a meat-and-potatoes man. So Mary kicks off her shoes, throws a robe over her clothes, and starts frying the pork chops and peeling the potatoes. Mary has become a Rescuer on the triangle. She is taking care of John because she thinks she should. Further, she discounts John's ability to take care of himself. She defines John as a Victim on the triangle.

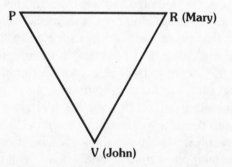

After thumbing through the mail, John comes into the kitchen and says to Mary, "Want some help, sweetie?" Mary wants some help, but because she thinks it's her job to do the cooking (this is one of Mary's script messages), she says to John, "Go ahead and relax; you've had a hard day, too." John ignores the word "too," which is a signal that Mary also has had a hard day. John goes to the den to read the paper. (John's script calls for him to be taken care of by a woman.)

By telling John to go relax, Mary has discounted her own needs (she also needs to sit down or at least have some help), and she has discounted John's ability to take care of himself (he is perfectly capable of helping her). Mary has once again defined herself as a Rescuer and her husband as a Victim.

As Mary stands in the kitchen peeling potatoes and frying pork chops, she starts to feel irritated and thinks to herself, "Why is it my job to wait on him? Why can't he wait on himself!" When John walks into the kitchen to read Mary an article he has run across in the newspaper, Mary says sarcastically, "I wish I had time to read the paper the way you men do." Mary has moved from the Rescuer role to the Persecutor role on the triangle.

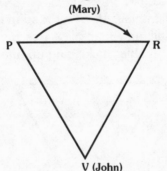

Now it's John's move. John can choose to take the bait, become a Persecutor, and say, "You women are all alike. I said I'd help!" Or he can become a Rescuer and say, "Mary, you go sit down and I'll finish cooking the dinner." If he becomes Mary's Rescuer, he may, however, start to feel like a Victim himself when he has to prepare the rest of the dinner alone.

The best course of action at this point is for John to say, "Let's do dinner together. I'll set the table and make the salad." By the same token, Mary can get herself off the triangle by saying, "I'd like to take you up on that offer of help now, John."

On first reading this, you might think that it was all Mary's fault. After all, if she had accepted her husband's offer of help in the first place, she wouldn't have gotten herself on the triangle. But John's question, "Want some help, sweetie?", was equally inappropriate. When two people both come home tired from working all day, both need to pitch in and prepare dinner.

Another way to look at this transaction is to see that John's question was Attention-Competitive. With "Want some help, sweetie?" John was covertly asking Mary to take care of him, and he was discounting that she, too, had worked all day.

On the Triangle with "What Do You Do with All the Money?"

In this next example you can see how easy it is to get on the triangle, and how fast one can move around on it. The setting again takes place in the kitchen.

Jim, after searching for something to eat, announces disgustedly, "There is never anything to eat around this joint. What do you do with all the money I give you for groceries?"

Joan, already feeling frustrated from cleaning up two previous messes of Jim's, says sarcastically, "That belly of yours doesn't look a bit undernourished to me."

In this situation, Jim plays Persecutor by making messes and not cleaning up after himself, and Joan plays Rescuer by cleaning up after Jim, who is perfectly capable of cleaning up after himself.

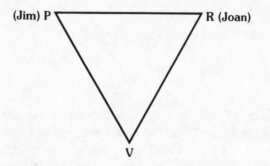

Jim then persecutes Joan further with his angry remark "What do you do with all the money I give you for groceries?" and Joan moves from Rescuer to Victim.

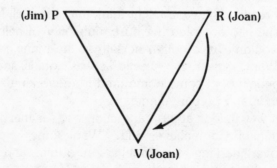

A second later another switch occurs as Joan moves from Victim to Persecutor with her remark about Jim's belly. And Jim moves to Victim.

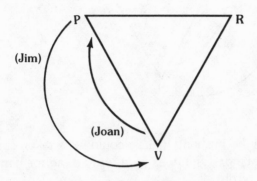

With each comment Joan or Jim moves on the triangle, and with each comment there is additional hurt and anger.

What's wonderful is that either Jim or Joan could choose to get off of the triangle at any time. Jim could say, "I'm sorry about that crack I made about money," or, "Come on, I don't want to fight. Let's get out of here and take a walk." Or Joan might say, "Let's not fight, and I'm sorry I said that about your belly."

On the Triangle with the Husband's Friend

One couple I was seeing in counseling brought me this example of how they got on the triangle. They had gone to a party, and one of the husband's business friends took a potshot at the wife. At the time neither of them said anything. But when they got home, the wife complained to her husband about how lousy the friend's comment was. Instead of defending his wife and saying, "Yeah, that was a lousy thing to say," the husband persecuted his wife by telling her she was too sensitive. To add fuel to the fire, he rescued his friend by saying that his friend probably had had a bad day.

Later that night the wife got her own licks in and she became the Persecutor. When her husband approached her sexually, she pulled away and said, "Anyone who is as sensitive as I am couldn't possibly have sex when they're feeling aggravated with their husband." At this point the wife moved from Victim to Persecutor and the husband moved from Persecutor to Victim.

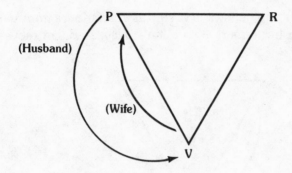

In this situation the husband initially could have taken care of his wife's feelings by saying, "That was a crummy thing for him to say. You must have felt terrible."

The wife, on the other hand, could have refused sex by saying, "I need a little time to dissipate my feelings. Maybe tomorrow morning . . ."

The important thing here: either spouse can get off the triangle.

On the Triangle with Children

If you have children, being on the triangle seems to be inevitable. Mom corrects one of the children, and Dad jumps in and says to Mom, with the child standing right there, "Come on, Mom, he's only young once. And besides, boys will be boys." Dad in this instance has become Mom's Persecutor and the child's Rescuer, while Mom has become the Victim.

Or a child gets in trouble at school for cheating on a test. When the parents find out, they both feel angry at the child and embarrassed by the situation. As they discuss the problem, one parent blames the other for the child's lack of values, and suddenly one parent has become the Persecutor and the other parent has moved to Victim. And the child's behavior is no longer the focus. Another way to look at this transaction is to see that the issues have switched from the child's behavior to which parent is responsible.

Other Versions of Being on the Triangle

Here are a few more transactions where husbands and wives become Rescuers, Victims, and Persecutors.

—Victim wife says, "I just can't get it all together today." Persecutor husband says, "Now tell me, when have you ever been able to get it all together?"

—Husband says, "How about going to breakfast with me tomorrow?" Wife says, "I'd love to, but I've got an appointment with my therapist." Husband, who hates his wife's seeing a therapist, turns Persecutor and says, "By all means, don't break your appointment with your shrink, because if anyone needs one, you certainly do." Wife turns Persecutor and responds, "Living with you, who wouldn't need a shrink!"

—After looking at the bank statement for forty-five seconds, Victim wife says, "I'll never be able to figure this thing out." Rescuer husband says, "Here, let me do it for you." Later that same day Victim wife turns Persecutor and says, "Boy, you sure made a mess of this statement."

—Victim husband says, "These three kids are driving me crazy. I can't stand it." Rescuer wife says, "I'll take them grocery shopping with me. Then you can get some rest and watch the football game in peace." We all know that when Rescuer wife gets to the grocery store and tries to shop with three children, she's going to start feeling like a Victim.

TEST TIME

Now it's time to take a test. Grab your pencil and fill out the following three stories. Write an R for Rescuer, a V for Victim, or a P for Persecutor. The number you get right will indicate how well you understand what's been presented in this chapter.

● Situation 1

Al walks into the kitchen and asks his wife, Rose, if she would be willing to get a new license for their car since the old one is about to expire. Rose, already not sure how she is going to finish everything she has scheduled, agrees to get the license. Enter Rose as (1) _____ on the triangle. Al, assuming that everything has been taken care of, forgets about the conversation until one afternoon when a policeman pulls him over and gives him a summons for expired license plates.

Enter Al as a (2) _____ on the triangle. He drives home, storms into
the house, waves the ticket in Rose's face, and tells her how incom-
petent she is. Al has become a (3) _____ on the triangle, and Rose
has become a (4) _____. Rose, not about to take Al's abuse lying
down, says sarcastically, "Listen, Al, if you'd do a little more around
here, I wouldn't have so much to do myself, and then I wouldn't have
forgotten the license." Rose again has moved on the triangle; now
she's a (5) _____ and Al has moved from (6) _____ to (7) _____.

● Situation 2

Passive Aggressive husband sits and watches his wife make dinner.
As she brings the food to the table, he says, "Do I have time to get
into my sweatsuit, or do I have to be uncomfortable and eat dinner in
this three-piece suit?" Although presenting himself as a (8) _____,
he's really the (9) _____ on the triangle.

If the wife is a Caretaker, she probably will respond as a (10)
_____ and say, "Go ahead and change; I'll put the food back in the
oven for a few minutes." If the wife is a Corrector, she is likely to
respond as a (11) _____ and say, "Why in heaven's name didn't you
change before now?"

● Situation 3

As Ed and Joan are getting ready for work, Joan says, "I've been
thinking. We are really going to be tight on time tonight. So instead
of my fixing dinner, let's just fast-food it before the ball game." Ed
says, "Well, I'm still trying to diet, so how about if you just make a
salad." Joan agrees.

After work Joan remembers that she doesn't have enough greens
to make a salad, so she stops at the supermarket. Then she rushes
home, changes her clothes, and fixes the salad. Five minutes before
they are scheduled to leave for the game, Ed walks in and says, "Oh,
you decided not to fast-food it?" Enter Ed as (12) _____ on the
triangle. Joan responds to Ed's comment by yelling, "You idiot! You
told me you wanted a salad for dinner. You're always pulling a switch."
Joan is now a (13) _____ on the triangle. Ed says nothing to Joan.
Instead he quietly goes upstairs to change his clothes. Ed perceives
himself as a (14) _____, while in reality Ed is a (15) _____. When
Ed comes downstairs, Joan, feeling guilty for her outburst, says, "I'll

drive and you can eat your salad on the way to the game." Joan has become a (16) _____ on the triangle, and she defines Ed as a (17) _____. Ed responds sarcastically and says, "No thanks. I'm no longer hungry." Ed's comment keeps him on the triangle as a (18) _____.

● Answers

(1) *R*   (2) *V*   (3) *P*   (4) *V*   (5) *P*   (6) *P*   (7) *V*   (8) *V*   (9) *P*   (10) *R*
(11) *P*   (12) *P*   (13) *P*   (14) *V*   (15) *P*   (16) *R*   (17) *V*   (18) *P*

Well, how did you do? If you have seventeen or eighteen correct answers, give yourself a gold star, since you clearly understand the Drama Triangle. If you have less than seventeen correct, you may want to review this chapter.

WE'RE ALL SUSCEPTIBLE

As you can see, being on the triangle does not make for a good relationship and it causes a lot of unnecessary pain in your marriage. Yet everybody gets on the triangle from time to time because we're human and we make mistakes. At the same time, it's relatively easy to get off the triangle, because once you know you're on the triangle, you can decide to move off.

Take Ed and Joan for example. Ed got on the triangle as a Persecutor when he "forgot" that he had specifically asked Joan to make him a salad. As soon as he saw the salad, or as soon as Joan so impolitely reminded him of the salad, he could have apologized. Thus he would have gotten off the triangle. Instead he decided to make Joan pay for her anger by pouting. When he came downstairs and Joan apologized for her angry outburst, Ed could have apologized also and then eaten the salad. He could have made a choice not to be on the triangle. Instead he once again *made a choice* to stay on the triangle.

You can easily avoid the Rescuer role on the triangle by taking both *your* wants and needs and those of your mate into consideration, and only then deciding if you want to do something for the other person. You can also avoid the Rescuer role by not seeing others as helpless and by giving yourself permission to say no to something that you do not want to do.

You can avoid the Victim role on the triangle by not seeing yourself as helpless or presenting yourself as helpless to your spouse.

You can avoid the Persecutor role by not using put-downs, guilt, sarcasm, pouting (all forms of anger) to get your own way, and by taking responsibility and apologizing when you do mess up.

You can avoid the triangle. Mostly, it's a matter of choice.

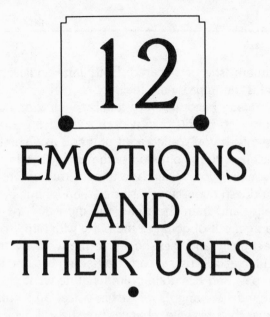

EMOTIONS AND THEIR USES

MANEUVERING WITH FEELINGS

Just as you were scripted for a particular position in life, you were also scripted to *feel* a certain way. In one family everyone gets angry. In another family everyone feels sad. And in a third family the members opt for feeling righteous. Everyone thinks that what they feel in a certain situation is the "appropriate" feeling, but mostly we feel what we have been taught or have been given permission to feel.

I see this all the time when I do group therapy. One member will be outraged about something, while another member says, "Gee, if I were you, I would have felt hurt." Another member sits there and feels scared by the angry display that she has just witnessed.

Because Jane grew up in a family where everyone was quick to anger, she most likely feels angry when something happens that calls for feelings. If someone cuts Jane off on the highway, she feels angry. If her husband fails to call her when he is going to be late, she feels angry. If her husband makes a sarcastic comment, she gets angry.

On the other hand, Betty's family taught her to feel scared. So when someone cuts her off on the highway, she feels scared. If her husband fails to call her when he is going to be late, or makes a sarcastic comment, she gets scared. Both Jane and Betty think that what they feel is the appropriate feeling.[1]

When a person becomes very familiar with a particular feeling, he learns to use it to get his own way. I always tell people it's a little like playing tennis. If you played a lot of tennis as a child and you've become proficient, you're going to use that ability to win on the tennis court. Why wouldn't you? The same thing is true of feelings.

A person doesn't consciously sit down and think, "Ah-ha . . . I'll get overly angry and then she'll give me my way," or, "I'll act sad and then I can get out of going to the party with him," or, "I'll make my spouse feel guilty and then he'll give me what I want." Without thinking, he automatically uses a particular feeling because it has worked so well in the past and has gotten him what he wanted.

If a husband gets angry, raises his voice, and huffs and puffs louder or longer than his wife, chances are she will back down to get him to stop being so angry with her. More than likely he will have his way. If, on the other hand, a woman is forever feeling down in the dumps, her husband may not expect too much of her. He may even shower her with love and attention to shore her up. Inadvertently her unhappiness may get her more than she realizes.

Anger

One woman I saw in marriage counseling said that anytime she had an argument with someone and told her husband about it, he would become twice as angry at the person. The woman would end up feeling as though she had to take care of her husband and calm him down, instead of being able to talk the incident through with him and being taken care of by her husband. This man was using his anger to shift the attention away from his wife and to himself. Another way to interpret this situation is to see that the husband was being Attention-Competitive, competing with his wife over who was going to get taken care of, him or her.

The situation was corrected when the wife was able to identify what was going on and explain it to her husband. The couple then made a pact that when the wife was irritated or angry with someone, he would not become angry, but instead would listen and try to comfort her. If he did become irritated when he heard the story, he would not become *more* angry than his wife.

In addition to escalating anger to get their mates to take care of them, some spouses become more angry than their mates in order to take control and justify doing what they want to do in the relationship.

For example, Joan feels angry at Tom because he didn't do what he had promised. When Joan confronts Tom, he becomes angry at her, except his anger is greater than her anger. In the end Joan backs down because Tom is more angry than she is. Tom has used his anger to redefine the issue. Or, one could say he is Control-Competitive, competing with Joan over who's going to be in charge and have the last word.

When I work with a couple who have this particular problem, I suggest that the spouse who feels intimidated by such a display of anger say to herself, "He is escalating his anger—in order to scare me—so he has control."

Saying this to yourself in the midst of a disagreement has a twofold effect:

1. You'll feel less scared because you're focusing on the process that is occurring.

2. Your spouse will actually "feel" that you are not as scared, which will have a calming effect on him.

Then, when each of you is more in control again, you might say, "Let's go back to the original issue that I brought up."

One man I worked with in therapy escalated his anger from day one of his marriage. He would absolutely "go wild" if his wife said anything that was the least bit critical of him. In the beginning of their therapy, they constantly fought over chores and his consistent failure to do what he had agreed to do. I still remember a particular incident. One Sunday, after his wife pointed out that he hadn't done his chores, including cleaning the goldfish bowl, the husband became so outraged that he picked up the bowl, marched to the bathroom, and poured its contents, including the poor goldfish, down the toilet.

Eventually this husband did learn to control his anger and not escalate when he was confronted. He attributed this successful handling of anger to the technique of saying to himself, "Nobody needs to get that angry." He repeated this phrase three thousand times a day for two months. (See chapter 9.) His wife, on the other hand, learned not to become so scared of his anger. When he was marching around the house acting like a spoiled brat, she would say, "You need to get in control of yourself," or, "You're trying to scare me into backing down about the chores." These statements were helpful to both of them.

To verbalize what was happening, the wife had to *think* about what was going on, which meant she wasn't allowing herself to be overwhelmed with her own scared feelings. For the husband, the statement "You're trying to scare me into backing down" was like a flashing red light that helped him slow down and get himself back in control.

People also escalate their anger to try to get their point across. This often happens with a woman who is a Caretaker and does far more in the relationship than her husband. She'll start out by complaining about all the things she does in the marriage, and soon she'll be off and running about all the things he doesn't do. Her points may be valid, but because she gets herself so out of control, her husband is able to discount her by focusing on her "nutsy" behavior, and not on *what* she is saying. She actually sabotages herself with too much anger.

One couple verbalized this phenomenon quite succinctly. The wife said, "I get too angry because he doesn't listen to what I say," to which the husband replied, "And I don't listen to what she says because she gets too angry."

Two additional side effects occur when the wife has her tantrum. First, the husband gets a lot of attention from his wife, and although the attention is negative, it is a form of recognition. As social scientists have proved many times over, negative attention is better than no attention at all. Second, because anger is an energizer, the woman is actually energized after the tantrum and often does the chores that her husband hasn't done. She continues playing out her script of doing everything, while supporting her husband's script to do as he pleases.

One woman figured out that every time she got overly tired and still had a lot to get done before going to bed, she would pick a fight with her husband. When the ruckus was over, she would have enough energy to go another two or three hours. She didn't realize these fights actually sustained her Caretaker position and her husband's Passive Aggressive position.

If you find that you are escalating your anger to get your point across, ask yourself how effective this maneuver has been for you.

Many people have told me that after they had a temper tantrum, their spouse made some changes. But within a week their spouse would be back to the same old behavior. So in the end, this maneuver didn't get them very far—except that they started disliking themselves because of these angry explosions.

If you've been having temper tantrums to get your point across and you're willing to try something different, start repeating two thousand times a day, "I don't need to yell and scream to get my point across." Saying this in your head for three or four weeks will help you keep yourself more in control when you talk with your spouse.

Another technique I use with people who get too angry is to suggest that, instead of yelling, "I'm furious . . . ," or, "I'm so mad at you . . . ," (statements that serve to escalate their anger), they substitute the phrase "I'm mildly annoyed." Imagine the wife standing in the kitchen screaming, "I'm mildly annoyed because you didn't put the trash out again," or, "I'm mildly annoyed because you woke me this morning." I gave one fellow this assignment, and every time he heard himself bellowing, "I'm mildly annoyed because you did such and such," he would break out laughing.

Another maneuver that spouses use against their mates is pouting, a more subtle form of anger. For example, the wife tells her husband she's irritated about something he did, and the husband responds by getting quiet and pouting. If the wife is sensitive to her husband's withdrawal, she'll start to feel guilty about what she said, and she'll try to cajole him into talking to her again. The original issue that she brought up with her husband falls by the wayside. It's like double jeopardy: The wife is irritated because her husband hasn't done something for her, and then she has to take care of him since he's irritated because she's irritated.

Another example is the wife who invites her husband to feel guilty by using a question with a hidden agenda. The husband and wife are shopping, and he finds a suit he likes. As they're waiting for alterations, she says, "Do you really think you need another new suit?" Instantly he starts to feel guilty because he hears the hidden agenda: "You don't need another suit." If he decides to buy the suit anyway, he'll feel guilty. If he puts the suit back, he'll have to deal with his own feelings of disappointment and anger. His wife's question has put him in a corner: Either way he decides to act, he feels guilty.

Another classic is the husband who doesn't want his wife to go out at night. The day she is to meet her friend for dinner and a movie, the husband puts on a long face, becomes quiet, and mopes around the house. The wife responds to her husband's behavior with feelings of guilt, and at 6:00 p.m. she telephones her friend and says she has a headache and can't make it.

The main reason guilt works is that the spouse who feels guilty is usually overly dependent on her mate for approval. If she doesn't do what her husband wants her to do, she feels guilty. She gives up what she wants in order to get back in her husband's good graces. The person who is most susceptible to feeling guilty is the Caretaker, because she needs to please at all times. The mate who is most prone to use guilt is the Passive Taker, who thinks he can't take care of himself and expects others to take care of him.

I worked with one woman who owned a deli with her husband. She was in an automobile accident and suffered nerve damage in both her neck and arm, and the doctor told her not to work. Her husband, however, thought she *should* work. She felt so guilty when she went against her husband's wishes, she went in to work even though the job aggravated her condition. When she started liking and respecting herself more, she was able to stop work without feeling guilty. Eventually her husband gave up his anger because it was no longer effective. She changed, and he changed as a result.

If you're susceptible to feeling guilty, make a pact with yourself that the next time you feel this way, you'll evaluate what your spouse wants you to do versus what you want to do. For example, you want to take a course given only in the evenings, and your spouse wants you home with him. If you don't take the course, you'll feel sad and disappointed; if you take the course, you'll feel guilty for leaving your spouse at home alone. Think about the advantages of taking the course versus staying home. If you decide to take the course, you're still going to experience some guilt. But each time you think through the issues and make a decision based on both your spouse's and your own wants, you'll be less susceptible to feeling guilty. You can also take your spouse's feelings into consideration and perhaps do something special another evening. Also, talk about what you're feeling. Chances are he is only vaguely aware that he is subtly pressuring you to stay home. I have found that people who feel guilty are often their own worst enemies.

Fear and Depression

People frequently use scared feelings to *avoid* doing something or to *justify* doing something. For instance, a husband is offered a promotion, but the job requires some travel. The wife says she's too scared to stay home alone while he travels. Underlying this feeling of fear, however, is the suspicion that her husband will be unfaithful. On the other hand, the husband is concerned about this job and his ability to handle it. In the end, he turns down the job because his wife is afraid to stay home alone. Both spouses support the wife's feeling scared in order to avoid dealing with their own insecurities. Their behavior is also a perfect setup for a future game of If-It-Weren't-for-You ("If it weren't for you being afraid to stay home alone, I'd have a better job and be making more money").

In this situation either the husband or the wife needs to take the risk and talk about his or her own insecurities. When one spouse is willing to share concerns, the other spouse often gets courage and follows suit.

Another husband learned as a child that if he walked around the house looking sad, his parents didn't expect much of him, and he was left to do as he pleased. Now that he's married, he walks around the house feeling sad, and his wife responds by not making too many demands of him. After all, what can you expect of someone who's depressed all the time? The wife expects little of her husband, so she also expects that he'll make few demands of her. His depression actually serves both of them in negative ways. They avoid closeness, something they both fear.

If you're the mate who often feels sad or scared, ask yourself what you get from feeling this way. Is it extra attention, a way to get out of work, a cover-up for another insecurity that is more painful to deal with, or simply a bad habit learned long ago? Once people know what they get from feeling a certain way, they are often able to deal with this problem, and thus stop maneuvering with their favorite feeling.*

If it's your mate who often feels sad and scared, you also need to do some mental gymnastics. Figure out how you support this feeling and what *you* might be getting because your mate feels this way.

Happiness

Although I've focused on the more unpleasant feelings that people subconsciously use to manipulate their mates, a person may present herself as constantly happy as a way to cover up or avoid dealing with the unpleasant things that are occurring in her life.

For instance, one woman I saw was always happy and everything was "wonderful" despite the fact that her husband drank constantly and often missed work and they teetered on the brink of financial disaster. She was using her "I'm so happy" routine to avoid facing these painful problems. What was interesting was that when she said, "I'm so happy," I didn't feel her happiness, nor did anyone else around her. When she started talking about these problems and she gave herself permission to feel hurt and anger and fear and sadness, her happiness, too, seemed more authentic.

A CHECKLIST TO DETERMINE
YOUR FAVORITE FEELING

Many couples manipulate each other with their favorite feelings, so it's helpful to know what your favorite emotion is. Once you recognize it, you can stop using it destructively.

The following questions were designed to help you identify your favorite emotion and to determine how you may be using this feeling inappropriately in your relationship. The answers to the questions have once again been filled in to help familiarize you with using this tool. Later you will be asked to fill in a set of your own answers.

Mike's Favorite Feeling Checklist

1. **What feeling do I have most often in my marriage?**
   "I often feel downtrodden."

2. **What does my mate do to help me feel this way?**
   "She continually criticizes me."

3. **How do I act or behave when I feel this way?**
   "I look sad and am quiet. I watch television, sleep, or read. When I'm sad, I don't have to do the chores I've agreed to do."

4. **What hidden benefit is there for my mate when I feel this way?**
"She thinks that she's better than me. Also, when I don't do my chores, she stops doing her chores."

5. **What hidden benefit is there for me when I feel this way?**
"I get out of chores and get taken care of. Because after a few days of neither of us doing chores and not talking, my wife can't stand it. She goes on a clean-up campaign. And she acts extra nice to me."

It's pretty clear that Mike plays Passive Taker, whereas his wife plays Corrector and Caretaker.

Linda's Favorite Feeling Checklist

Linda is a Caretaker, and her husband is a Passive Aggressive. Here's how she answered the Favorite Feeling Checklist:

1. **What feeling do I have most often in my marriage?**
"Anger."

2. **What does my mate do to help me feel this way?**
"He doesn't do what he promises me he will do. We make agreements, and then he doesn't keep his word."

3. **How do I act or behave when I feel this way?**
"I get angry and stomp around the house. If someone saw me at the height of one of my tantrums, they'd probably think I'd gone off my rocker."

4. **What hidden benefit is there for my mate when I feel this way?**
"He gets a lot of attention. First he gets negative attention because of my yelling and screaming, and then I give him positive attention trying to make up to him because I'm so embarrassed about my behavior."

5. **What hidden benefit is there for me when I feel this way?**
"I get to be critical of my husband, which I normally don't give myself permission to be. I get energized by the argument. One time I cleaned every closet in the house after one of my tantrums. And usually my husband does do a few more things around the house after I've been angry with him, at least for a few days."

It's clear that Linda and her husband get a lot of hidden benefits from her anger. What's sad is that most of these "benefits" are destructive to the relationship.

Your Favorite Feeling Checklist

Now it's your turn to answer the questions.

1. What feeling do I have most often in my marriage? _____

_____

2. What does my mate do to help me feel this way? _____

_____

3. How do I act or behave when I feel this way? _____

_____

4. What hidden benefit is there for my mate when I feel this way?

_____

5. What hidden benefit is there for me when I feel this way? _____

_____

Notice that the hidden benefits for both you and your spouse are reinforcements of your script messages and your script positions.

TRYING ON OTHER FEELINGS

What most people come to understand in therapy is that the continual use of one feeling in a relationship may have a controlling effect on their spouse, at least for a time, but at some point this feeling loses its effectiveness and may even be the undoing of the marriage. Most spouses today are simply not willing to be beaten down by anger or controlled by pouting week after week, year after year. They are not willing to put up with a mate who is too scared and depressed to enjoy life. So be aware of your favorite feeling and be careful not to overwork it.

Also, if you expect to live up to your full potential, you'll want to give yourself permission to experience all feelings and not get trapped into experiencing only one or two emotions.

People often will ask, "How can I learn to feel more than I'm scripted to feel?" The question is a valid one. You experience a particular feeling because that is the emotion you learned. And when something happens that calls for an emotion, you are automatically going to experience that feeling internally.

The way you change is first to deal with the problem externally. The next time you feel internally angry, try on a different feeling and say out loud, "I feel sad," or, "I feel depressed." If your favorite emotion is downtrodden, substitute, "I feel mildly annoyed." Each time you verbalize an emotion different from your favorite feeling, you are giving yourself permission to experience another feeling. Although this exercise may sound a little farfetched, it works. It's the very way you learned to feel your favorite emotion long ago.

So get going and feel happy and sad and scared and depressed and giggly and pleased and concerned and anxious and creative and irritable and silly and ridiculous and loving and caring and kind and generous. You deserve to feel a variety of emotions. You deserve to feel life!

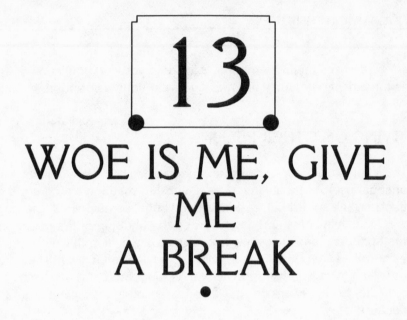

13

WOE IS ME, GIVE ME A BREAK

Maybe you have come to the point where you're thinking, "No wonder we have a poor marriage—between my mate and myself, we do everything wrong. We compete for who's going to run the show. We compete for attention. We're always on the Drama Triangle. And we both try to manipulate each other with our feelings. There's no way we're going to change all this stuff. It's too much."

It's true. I've been giving you a lot of information. And you won't change everything. But you don't have to. You do have to change some things, however, and if you focus on changing one or two things, other pieces will fall into place.

Suppose you've become aware that you are Control-Competitive (you compete with your wife over who's going to run the show) and that as a result you often correct your wife in front of friends. Now you make a decision to stop this annoying behavior; no matter how difficult it is, you promise you won't correct her in front of friends. Even if you have to bite your tongue. By sticking to this decision, you're also avoiding getting on the Drama Triangle. (When you correct your wife in public, you're a Persecutor and she's a Victim.) With the decision to stop correcting your wife in public, you're killing two birds with one stone.

Or suppose every time your wife gets angry at her mother, you turn around and get twice as angry at her mother. Clearly you are being Attention-Competitive (you are competing with your wife over who's going to get taken care of). Now that you recognize this about yourself, you decide that even though you will probably still get angry with your mother-in-law when you hear something she has done, you won't get more angry than your wife. Instead you will comfort your wife and take care of her. By making this decision, you are also avoiding getting on the Drama Triangle as a Persecutor. In addition, you are not maneuvering your wife with your anger, which is probably your favorite emotion. With this decision to stop getting more angry than your wife, you are killing three birds with one stone.

Don't put it on yourself that you have to analyze and change all your behaviors or change them all at once.

Remember, counseling takes a lot longer than it takes to read this book. Also, it takes time to incorporate this information, so pace yourself. Chip away at those issues that seem to be the easiest to tackle and those that cause the most problems in your marriage. As you clean up these behaviors, other behaviors will change.

Another thing to keep in mind is that a lot of what we have been focusing on are those behaviors that cause problems in your marriage. At the same time, you have some good things going in your relationship. So don't discount all the good. Or as my grandmother used to say, "Now, don't go throw the baby out with the bath water."

Also, you have a lot of the most difficult material behind you. Thus you'll probably find yourself zipping through the next three chapters, so hang in there.

STROKES

ACCENTUATE THE POSITIVE,
ELIMINATE THE NEGATIVE

During the entire marriage counseling process, I'm always asking a person to focus on the stroking pattern in her marriage. I want her to recognize when she gives a positive stroke and when she gives a negative stroke and the impact that these two very different kinds of strokes have on her marriage. I want her to be cognizant of how often she smiles and says "I love you" versus the putdowns and the sarcastic comments she makes. I expect her to know what her mate's favorite strokes are, as well as the strokes she enjoys receiving most. The number of strokes and the kind of strokes that are exchanged in the relationship play a significant part in the happiness of the marriage.

Positive Strokes

A positive stroke is a sign of recognition that carries the message, "You're okay." This message can come in the form of a hug, a pat on the back, a playful wink, a sexy pinch, a smile, a verbal compliment, or a similar act.

Some positive strokes are merely maintenance strokes. "Hello" and "Goodbye" are considered maintenance strokes. Other positive strokes enhance a person's sense of self-worth. Saying "I love you" and "You're so special to me" fall within this category. Other positive strokes are based on a person's competency, such as "You're a terrific cook," and, "I like the way you planted that flower bed." Some positive strokes are expressions of appreciation; for example, "Thanks for mailing my package and stopping by the hardware store." Other positive strokes are expressions of affection, as, "You have the greatest laugh," and, "I love your dimples." And some positive strokes take the form of doing something for one's spouse, as in the case of the man who says, "You go sit and relax; I'll clean up the kitchen."

Suppose a husband smiles and says to his wife, "You look beautiful." As he says this, he gives her a little hug and adds, "I love you." A few minutes later he says, "By the way, thanks for picking up my shirts from the cleaners." His statements "You look beautiful" and "I love you," as well as his smile and the hug, are referred to as unconditional strokes;* strokes he's giving his wife just for *being.* The wife didn't have to do anything for her husband to get these strokes. They were free. His comment "Thanks for picking up my shirts" is referred to as a conditional stroke,* a stroke he gives his wife for *doing.* He gave his wife this stroke because she went to the cleaners to pick up his shirts.

Note also that this husband gave his wife three verbal strokes: "You look beautiful," "I love you," and "Thanks for picking up my shirts." He also gave her two nonverbal strokes: the smile and the hug. In addition, the hug was a physical stroke.

While I was writing this book, my husband would often bring me a cup of coffee. He would walk over to my desk, put his hand on my shoulder, and say, "How's it going?" The cup of coffee, the "How's it going?", and his hand on my shoulder were all unconditional strokes. His hand on my shoulder was also a physical stroke. Even though I liked it when he asked "How's it going?" and I enjoyed a cup of hot coffee, his hand on my shoulder felt the very best to me.

The reason I'm making a point of differentiating between whether a stroke is verbal or nonverbal, unconditional or conditional, and sometimes physical is that certain strokes carry more weight with certain individuals.

Some spouses put hugs (a physical stroke) on the top of their list as the kind of stroke they want most. Others like to be told, "I love you," (a verbal, unconditional stroke). Some mates discount both these types of strokes but revel in the conditional strokes of "Your dinner was delicious," or, "You did a fine job trimming that bush."

The strokes we like to hear are often those strokes that were given to us as children. Caretakers and Correctors seem to be most attuned to conditional strokes and often discount unconditional strokes. However, as they are able to move out of their script positions, they often become more attuned to strokes for being.

● Your Spouse's Favorite Stroke

One woman I saw in marriage counseling used to accuse her husband of not loving her. He would respond to this accusation by defending himself with a list of things he had done that showed he did love her. The problem for this couple was that she wanted him to give her hugs and whisper sweet nothings. He, on the other hand, helped with the dishes and kept the yard looking terrific. He was giving her the kind of strokes he would have liked to receive, but not the kind that she valued most.

Often a spouse will give a stroke that he wants, and he'll forget about or lose sight of whom the stroke is really intended for. One fellow was forever giving his wife lavish gifts of jewelry and clothing. In addition, he often gave her these gifts in public. He would have the waiter bring a beautifully wrapped package to their table. Or he would tell her to block off her schedule for a week and whisk her away to some exotic place. Every five or six months this fellow would come up with something spectacular, ostensibly for his wife. But in reality he was pleasing himself. What he didn't do was arrive home when he said he would, pay attention to her when she talked, make love to her when she wanted to, or take into account what might please her on a daily basis.

Unfortunately, many spouses are not aware of their mate's favorite strokes.

Here's a quick exercise to help you get in touch with the types of strokes your spouse enjoys. Make a check mark next to the items that seem to appeal especially to your mate.

☐ Holding hands.
☐ Going for a walk together.
☐ Having a drink together.
☐ Keeping the checkbook balanced.
☐ Dancing.
☐ Shopping together.
☐ Finding a love note under the pillow.
☐ Bringing home a surprise.
☐ Fixing dinner or a favorite dessert.
☐ Hearing "I love you."
☐ Receiving flowers.

- [ ] Making love.
- [ ] Having the house straightened.
- [ ] Keeping the lawn looking nice.
- [ ] Receiving compliments on his looks.
- [ ] Taking a shower together.
- [ ] Being read to.
- [ ] Getting a backrub.

- [ ] Being approached sexually.
- [ ] Having dinner out.
- [ ] Wrestling on the floor.
- [ ] Playing cards together.
- [ ] Receiving compliments on her achievements.
- [ ] Listening to him or her play the piano.
- [ ] Having a conversation.
- [ ] Having the bed turned down.

If you're not in touch with the types of positive strokes your husband or wife likes, consider the way he or she strokes you. A person often will give the very strokes he wants to receive. A more direct way to approach this issue is to ask your spouse directly, "What makes you feel taken care of by me?" or, "What kinds of compliments do you like to hear from me?" or, "When do you feel most loved by me?" These questions might seem strange, but many people live with each other for years without knowing exactly the kinds of strokes their spouse enjoys the most. And, although your spouse might be surprised by such a question, she surely will be pleased.

● Your Favorite Stroke

Another thing you might be surprised to learn is that you may not be aware of the strokes that *you* like to receive from your spouse. People who have the script messages "Work hard" and "Achieve" or "Don't feel" and "Don't think" are often unaware of what kinds of strokes they want. Caretakers and Passive Takers rarely know what strokes feel the best to them. If you're not sure of your favorite stroke, become more attuned to yourself. When your mate gives you a stroke, see how you feel inside. As you become more tuned in to yourself, you'll be able to identify what feels so-so, what feels good, and what feels gr-r-e-at.

If you're not getting the kinds of strokes you want from your spouse, take the risk and tell him or her what you would like. Years ago I had an old cartoon by Jules Feiffer hanging in my office. In the first frame the husband and wife were seated at the kitchen table and the wife was looking rather disgusted. In the next picture he asked her what was wrong. By the third frame she was telling him that she was angry because he hadn't passed the salt. In the fourth frame he responded, "But you didn't ask me to pass it." If this story rings a bell with you, take the risk and tell your mate the kinds of strokes you enjoy most.

Negative Strokes

When a spouse is not being recognized and stroked positively in a marriage, he or she will often go after a negative stroke. The reason is that everyone *needs* to be stroked, without exception. We all must be recognized.

Transactional analysts have a saying that if a person is not stroked, his spinal cord will shrivel and he will die. That is often why, if a spouse is not receiving enough positive strokes, she will start a fight to assure herself of some negative strokes. Also, if your spouse makes some changes and then you don't give her any positive strokes for them, or enough positive strokes, she'll go back to her old annoying behavior. At least with this annoying behavior she'll get some recognition, and even if the recognition is negative, negative strokes are far better than no strokes at all.

As I think of negative strokes, I'm always reminded of Faulkner's line, "Between grief and nothing I will take grief."[1] This is the reason why couples who fight day after day and exchange one nasty comment after another often stay together. They would rather suffer the pain of negative strokes than the pain of no strokes at all.

All negative strokes carry the message "You're not okay." Criticism, sarcastic remarks, name-calling, a dirty look, pushing, hitting, and the like are all negative strokes. Like positive strokes, negative strokes can be verbal or nonverbal, unconditional or conditional, and sometimes physical.

For example, a wife says to her husband, "Boy, you sure made a mess of the checkbook this month." Then she pats him on the head and says, "Didn't you, baldy?" Her comments are both verbal strokes, whereas patting him on the head is a nonverbal physical stroke. The comment about the checkbook was conditional and the comment about his lack of hair was unconditional. All were negative strokes.

Then there's the husband who says to his wife as she's dressing, "You know, since you've been going to that aerobics class, I think those saddlebags on your legs have actually increased, if that's possible. Ha ha." His comment is a verbal, unconditional negative stroke, as is his laughter.

Here are a few more examples of negative strokes:

- "Why don't you just give up and admit you're not mechanically inclined?"
- Don't tell me you're not wearing gloves in this weather!"
- Husband gives wife a present, and she says, "I see you bought me another dust collector."
- Wife comes home from the hairdresser, and husband says, "Don't tell me you spent money for *that*."
- Husband comes home from the barber, and wife says, "Who butchered you?"
- Wife feels sensitive about her age, particularly because she is three years older than her husband. On her birthday her husband gives her a card that reads on the outside, "You're forty," and when she opens it up it says, "And I'm not."

It's truly sad when you think of how many negative strokes some people give their spouse. Yet if their spouse were killed in an accident, they would mourn for months or even years.

It also saddens and still surprises me just how often people get into it physically. They push each other, and slap each other's faces, and throw things at one another, and even spit at each other.

I've worked with a wife who said she pulled her husband's glasses off, slapped his face, and kicked him in the shins. He, on the other hand, has dragged her through the house by her arms, shaken her as hard as possible, and pinned her against the wall. I know one husband who took a grocery cart and rammed it into the back of his wife at the grocery store, and another who purposely pushed his wife down the basement steps. All these people are well-educated, respected professionals. They work hard, play hard, and are law-abiding citizens. But behind their front doors they abused their spouses.

If this kind of stroking goes on in your marriage, I *strongly* recommend that you seek help beyond this book from a marriage counselor. If you or your spouse cannot get in control of yourselves through counseling, then separate until such time as you can get in control.

No one should endure physical abuse. Nor should this type of behavior ever be modeled for children.

• The Mixed Stroke

Some strokes are a combination of positive and negative; they say "You're okay" and "You're not okay" at the same time. Because the positive message, no matter how positive, is tainted by the negative message, mixed strokes fall in the negative category. Sometimes these strokes carry the biggest wallop, because often you get the positive part first, and as you are basking in the compliment, you get zapped.

I still recall one such stroke that was given to me many years ago. I had just finished giving a workshop when one of the participants said, "One of the things I like so much about the way you work is that you're so stroking of people." I smiled and was about to say thank you when he added, "I just wonder, with all those strokes you give, if they're real or a form of manipulation."

Here are a few more examples of mixed strokes:

- "If I didn't love you, I wouldn't be telling you this right now, but . . ."

- "You know, you have great legs for someone your age."

- "Oh, she's a terrific cook, aren't you, darling? When she cooks, that is. Ha ha."

- "I like your suit all right, but the color sort of makes you look dead."

- "Joan was telling me that she really enjoyed you at the dinner party the other night, and she didn't think you tried to hog the conversation at all."

- "That style looks good on you—it hides your hips."

Reading these examples, you can see why the negative part far outweighs the positive.

Strokes and Scripting

The kinds of strokes a person expects, hears, and gives to his mate are largely determined by his script. If a man was told, "You'll never amount to anything," he's certainly not going to accept many positive strokes, because deep down he doesn't see himself as worthy. In addition, subconsciously he is going to seek out negative strokes that imply he is no good. He might be constantly late in order to invite his wife to be irritated with him, or he might procrastinate to get his wife to badger him, or he might drink too much to get a negative comment from her.

For example, Jeff grew up in a family where he was constantly criticized by his father, therefore receiving the script message "Be criticized by others." He followed this message by marrying a very critical woman. Eleven years later he divorced her, turned around, and married another critical woman. He constantly badgered his children, who in turn were critical of him. And he procrastinated at work so the boss was always on his case.

In the beginning months of counseling, he would make agreements with his therapy group regarding what he would do the following week to change his behavior. Then he wouldn't keep the agreement. His group would get critical of him, and he would defend himself and get critical of the members of the group. He also discounted the positive strokes he did receive. If someone in the group told him that he had handled something well, he would laugh and start saying it was no big deal, which was his way of rejecting the positive stroke. Clearly his preference was for negative strokes, although on a conscious level he was unaware of how he constantly sought out the negative and rejected the positive.

A woman I worked with in marriage counseling was considered the rebellious one in the family as she was growing up. Often the strokes she received as a child not only were critical but were accompanied by a lot of anger. Through therapy she discovered that she picked fights with her husband to reexperience those angry strokes of the past.

What Happens When You're in Public

Sometimes the stroking that occurs when a couple is in public is a dramatic change from what happens when they're at home alone. It's as if the lights go on, the curtain goes up, and the performance begins. Some couples put on hurtful performances, where the digs fly back and forth. Other couples become more gracious and loving.

● License to Be Nasty

One man rarely said anything to his wife that was critical, but he didn't say much that was positive either. He was Passive Aggressive in the relationship, and his focus was himself. But when they were out in public, he almost always made some nasty remark about her. One of his favorite ploys was to tell a story about some flat-chested woman and then look at his wife and comment about how flat-chested she was. Underlying this hurtful remark was his own fear that he was not masculine enough. By blemishing his wife, he was masking his own feelings of inferiority.

Here are a few more comments I've heard at parties:

1. Friend to Wife: Are you becoming vegetarian?

   Wife: I've started. I rarely eat red meat anymore.

   Husband: So what was that you had on your plate last night?

2. Friend to Husband: How's your exercise program coming?

3. Wife to Friend: He weighs more than when he started.

   Wife to Friend: And then they offered me the job.

   Husband to Friend: I can't imagine why.

If your spouse takes a potshot at you in public, you can choose to ignore the comment altogether, you can give him the evil eye, you can bring it up when you get home, or you can call everyone's attention to the stroke by saying, "I don't like it that you choose to hurt me in front of our friends." This last alternative might sound harsh, but everyone in the room is already embarrassed, whereas your spouse, who has caused the problem, sits there feeling smug. Calling attention to his comment in public actually shifts some of the discomfort to him. If you decide to start using this technique, tell your mate what you intend to do. Sometimes the warning is enough to put an end to this obnoxious behavior.

If your spouse occasionally gives you a negative stroke when you're with friends, you might choose to let the issue go, since no one is perfect. However, if he or she gives you negative strokes with any regularity, you need to deal with them. Otherwise you are passively supporting this behavior.

● How Sweet It Is

Sometimes when a couple is out with their friends, they will give more positive strokes to each other than when at home alone. She'll put her arms around him, and he'll give her little kisses and tell everyone what a good wife she is. Each of them has been scripted to "look good in public."

Another variation is the husband who rarely talks to his wife when they are at home alone, but when they're with friends he turns on a switch and becomes the star. He is witty, talkative, and stroking, both to his wife and others. As soon as they're in the car, however, he reverts back to being quiet. He is following a script to "look good in public."

If either of these examples fits the way you and your mate behave, talk about this issue. Clearly you know how to stroke in a positive manner. The next step is to practice stroking each other for the benefit of the marriage instead of for the benefit of what others think. Also, since you already know how to stroke each other, you're already halfway there.

Your Response to Strokes

Unfortunately, negative strokes are accepted far more readily than positive strokes by most people because people tend to give a lot of power to others and often lose sight of the fact that they have a right to reject a negative stroke. Even when one knows the negative stroke he has been given is "hogwash," a negative stroke usually leaves its mark. Perhaps this idea is expressed best by Guareschi in *My Home, Sweet Home* when he wrote, "The man who offers an insult writes it in sand, but for the man who receives it it's chiseled in bronze."[2]

Also, a person sometimes may not accept a positive stroke because he doesn't feel as though he deserves it. It's the old "If you only knew me" routine. Or the stroke isn't the kind he's used to. If a person is hooked on negative strokes, he is less likely to hear positive strokes because they aren't as familiar. It's not that someone consciously says, "I won't accept this positive stroke I'm being given." It's that he's not attuned to positive strokes, and consequently he doesn't hear them.

• Accepting the Positive

When your spouse does give you a positive stroke, such as "I really like that suit on you," don't apologize and say, "Oh, *this* old thing." And don't discount his stroke by saying, "You've got to be kidding." Also, don't ask for another stroke by saying, "Are you sure?"

Say instead, "Thank you," after getting a stroke. The thank-you implies that you heard the stroke and you are taking it in.

• Rejecting the Negative

When you receive a negative stroke from your spouse, you can follow some of the following suggestions on how to respond. If your husband says you're getting fat, don't respond with how much weight he has put on, or how his appearance isn't so hot either. Don't put the criticism back on him. Also, don't redefine and change the subject to "You're always so critical." And don't escalate the situation by getting too angry or going for the bottom line with such statements as, "I never should have married you," or, "I don't know if I can stand living like this much longer."

Handle a negative stroke with active listening,[3] a technique that anyone who is married can certainly use from time to time. Simply reflect back to your mate what he has said to you verbally, and include how he must be feeling. With regard to the comment "You're getting fat," you might say, "I have put on weight, and I can see you're not very happy about it." Notice that this statement reflects back both the content of what your spouse has said, and his feelings on the issue. If he says, "The way you acted at the party was a little ridiculous, don't you think?" you might say, "You must be feeling annoyed because you didn't like the way I acted last night." Or if your spouse says, "Once again you cut me off when I was talking," you might say, "You're irritated because I didn't give you a chance to finish what you were saying, and I'm sorry."

You can see from these examples how active listening helps your spouse feel as though you've heard what he is saying. Also, active listening gives you time to hear what your mate is saying without escalating your feelings and becoming defensive.

I used to bum around with a fellow who taught courses on active listening. Sometimes this guy would drive me up the wall with his behavior, and in response to what he did, I'd get angry, and he'd stand there and "active-listen" me. And even though I knew what he was doing, I felt listened to and my anger did dissipate.

Another thing you can do when you get a negative stroke is to agree with that part of the criticism that is true. For example, if your wife says, "You never pay attention to me," you might say, "Sometimes I don't pay attention to you, and you must be feeling hurt by my lack of interest." This response will definitely have a calming effect on her. If your mate says, "Your hair looks terrible," and you also think it looks terrible, then agree with your mate and say, "Yeah, it does look pretty bad today." If, however, you don't agree with the comment "Your hair looks terrible," you can simply say, "I don't agree."

One thing I try to keep in mind when I get a negative stroke that I don't agree with is the following story:

> When a simpleton abused him, Buddha listened in silence; but when the man had finished, Buddha asked him: "Son, if a man declined to accept a present made to him, to whom would it belong?" The man answered: "To him who offered it." "My son," said Buddha, "I decline to accept your abuse, and request you keep it for yourself."[4]

If you're given a negative nonverbal stroke, such as a frown or a sigh or an ugly face, use your communication skills and say, "It looks as though you're disappointed with what I'm doing." Or, "It sounds as though you're disgusted that I ordered dessert when I'm already overweight. And it's true, I am overweight. However, this evening I'm going to have dessert." Note here that you've made the nonverbal comment verbal. You agreed with the criticism. Then you took responsibility and said what you were going to do.

THE MARITAL STROKE COUNT

It's now time to look at what strokes you give your spouse, whether these strokes are positive or negative, verbal or nonverbal, unconditional or conditional, and whether or not they are physical. I think you'll find the results of doing this exercise fascinating and very informative.

An Example

The following Marital Stroke Count has already been filled in. This will give you an example of how it works. The man who did this stroke count had been working on his marriage for four months. He has been married for twenty years.

STROKES I GAVE

	POSITIVE	NEGATIVE	VERBAL	NONVERBAL	UNCONDITIONAL	CONDITIONAL	PHYSICAL
DAY 1							
Told her I missed her.	X		X		X		
Gave her a hug.	X			X	X		X
Asked her how she was feeling.	X		X		X		
Commented about her haircut; said it looked good.	X		X			X	
DAY 2							
Offered to fix her coffee.	X		X		X		
Thanked her for picking up my pants from the cleaners.	X		X			X	
Asked her why she was wasting her time reading such a dumb book.		X	X		X		
Got angry and asked why for heaven's sake she didn't get stamps when she went to the post office to mail a package.		X	X			X	
DAY 3							
Said, "Good morning, honey."	X		X		X		
Kissed and hugged her.	X		X	X		X	

STROKES I GAVE

STROKES I GAVE	POSITIVE	NEGATIVE	VERBAL	NONVERBAL	UNCONDITIONAL	CONDITIONAL	PHYSICAL
Brought her a cup of coffee in bed.	X			X			
Called from work to say, "Hi."	X		X	X			
Offered to pick up dinner when she said she was feeling overwhelmed with her schedule.	X		X	X			
Said, "You look nice," and gave her a hug. (Note here: two in one.)	X		X	X		X	X
Nuzzled her neck.	X			X			X
Asked her if she wanted to join me on a walk.	X		X	X			
Brought her a glass of ice water.	X			X			
Woke up and said sarcastically, "Are you still working?"		X	X	X			
DAY 4							
Apologized for my comment last night about her working.	X		X	X			
Asked her if she wanted tea, and then brought it to her.	X		X	X			
Thanked her for buying my favorite cereal.	X		X		X		

Gave her a hug when I came home.	X				X	X	X
Asked her how work went today.	X		X		X	X	
Talked to her about a problem she was having at work.	X		X		X	X	
Gave her an article that I thought she might be interested in.	X			X	X	X	
Kissed her, hugged her, made love.	X			X	X	X	X

DAY 5

Brought her a glass of juice.	X				X	X	
Gave her a dirty look when she asked to borrow money for her lunch.		X		X	X	X	
Left without saying goodbye.		X		X	X	X	
Called to say I was sorry for this morning.	X		X		X	X	
Got into a fight with her while we were on the phone.		X	X	X	X	X	
Waited up for her to get home.	X			X	X	X	
Asked her how things had gone at her meeting.	X		X	X	X	X	
Sent her a funny card in the mail.	X			X	X	X	

DAY 6

Suggested she sleep in and promised to help with the grocery shopping.	X		X		X		

STROKES I GAVE

	PHYSICAL	CONDITIONAL	UNCONDITIONAL	NONVERBAL	VERBAL	NEGATIVE	POSITIVE
Had sex.	X			X			X
Fixed breakfast together and talked about the birds at the feeder.				X	X		X
Told her she had a green thumb.				X	X		X
Went shopping together. Suggested we have lunch out.				X	X		X
Gave her a backrub.	X			X			X
Sat with my arm around her as we watched television.	X			X			X

DAY 7

	PHYSICAL	CONDITIONAL	UNCONDITIONAL	NONVERBAL	VERBAL	NEGATIVE	POSITIVE
Took her to breakfast.				X			X
Told her dinner was delicious.			X		X		X
Listened to a presentation she was going to make.				X	X		X
Gave her a kiss before going to bed.	X			X			X
Told her what a nice weekend I had with her.				X	X		X
Total	10	5	41	20	27	6	40

● What "He" Found Out

The man who did this exercise became aware, after looking at his own Marital Stroke Count, that he gave his wife a lot of unconditional positive strokes, but he didn't give her many physical strokes. He realized that his wife's complaints about "You don't take care of me" were because she wasn't getting enough physical stroking. In the family in which she grew up, they not only did a lot of verbal stroking but a lot of physical stroking as well. Once this man increased the number of physical strokes he gave his wife, she felt more taken care of, and the marriage bloomed.

When the wife saw her husband's stroke count, she reported being "amazed" at the number of strokes she had actually discounted that her husband had given her during the week, and she became more tuned in to the verbal strokes she was getting.

An added advantage of this stroke count is that it shows that you can give your spouse a lot of positive strokes day to day that require little energy. The payoff for giving these strokes is a good relationship. It also helps you to see clearly how many negative strokes you give out. Some spouses have found the Marital Stroke Count so helpful that they use it daily. One man I worked with said, "It keeps me on my toes. When I do the stroke count every day, I'm aware of my behavior in the marriage."

I also think it's good to turn this idea around and do your spouse's stroke count. Instead of recording the strokes you gave, record the strokes you received. *Almost universally*, people find that their spouses give them far more positive strokes than they realize.

Your Marital Stroke Count

Now it's your turn. Fill out the stroke count and see how many and what kinds of strokes you actually give your partner.

I recommend that you keep the Marital Stroke Count for seven days. You should start by going back and recording the strokes you remember giving your spouse yesterday. Then continue with today, and record your strokes for the next five consecutive days. You might want to keep your stroke count on your night table and fill it in before you go to bed.

If you are absolutely unwilling to do the stroke count for seven days, at least fill it in for yesterday and today. Okay?

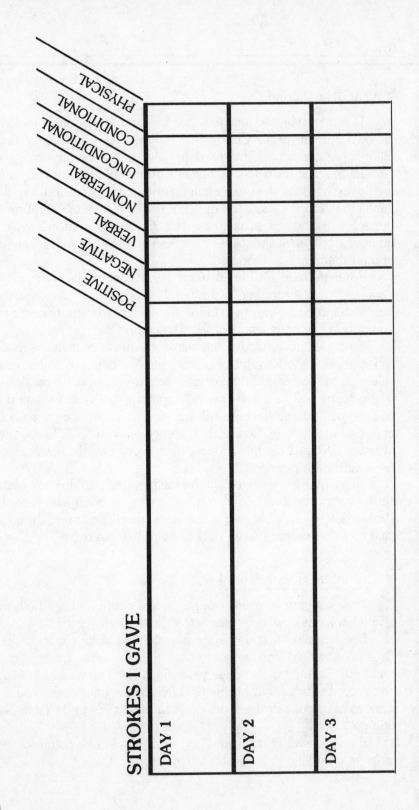

STROKES I GAVE

	POSITIVE	NEGATIVE	VERBAL	NONVERBAL	UNCONDITIONAL	CONDITIONAL	PHYSICAL
DAY 1							
DAY 2							
DAY 3							

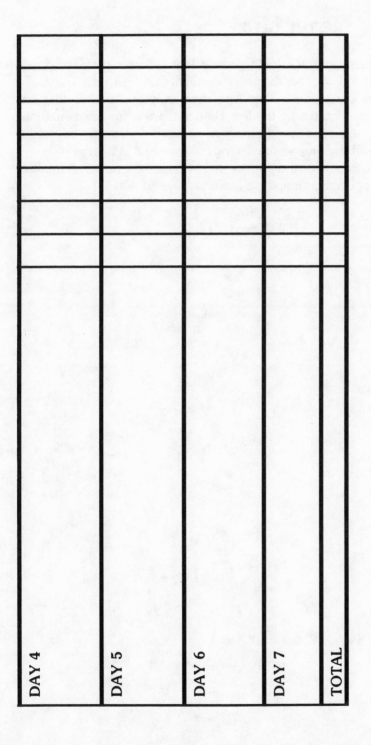

STROKES ARE THE GLUE

Positive strokes are the ingredient that makes a marriage good, while negative strokes are the very ingredient that destroys it. Generally a good rule of thumb is this: The more negative strokes that are exchanged in a marriage, the less chance there is for emotional intimacy. The more positive strokes that are exchanged, the better the marriage, and the greater the feelings of love and intimacy.

So . . . accentuate the positive and eliminate the negative. In other words, start giving your spouse more positive strokes.

OPTIONS
AND
ALTERNATIVES

WORKING TO A SOLUTION

As an individual or a couple I'm counseling move along in their therapy and are using the information and various techniques they have learned over the last four or five months, I find that I confront them less and throw fewer Nerf balls in the sessions. Both spouses look directly at the other as they speak, their communication is clear and specific, they take few potshots at each other, and they have moved beyond trying to prove that their spouse is at fault. With this new knowledge, the person not only starts looking at and understanding the relationship from a different frame of reference, but also has developed the ability to think about and solve problems differently. He thinks in terms of "What's *really* going on here?", "How am I playing into the problem?", and, "What are my options for solving this issue?" He uses all the information he has gained about himself, his spouse, and the relationship. And in most instances, he is able to come to a solution that satisfies both himself and his mate.

One Way to Solve a Problem

One process that an individual may use to solve his problem involves answering the following questions:

1. What do I want in concrete terms?
2. What does my spouse want in concrete terms?
3. Why does my mate feel this way?
4. What will I be giving up if I don't get my way?
5. Have I turned this problem into a power struggle, where having things go my way has become more important than the issue at hand?
6. What are some alternative solutions?

Some Examples

● To Sell or Not to Sell

One man I saw in therapy wanted to sell their house and move to a condominium where there would be less upkeep, utilities would be lower, and he would be free from yard work. The wife, however, loved their home and wasn't ready to move. Here's how this fellow answered the questions.

1. **What do I want in concrete terms?**
"I'd like to get the house ready to sell this spring and move to a condominium. This would allow me more free time since I wouldn't be so tied down doing maintenance and yard work. Also, it would give us a little more money each month because we wouldn't be paying so much in utility bills and taxes."

2. **What does my spouse want in concrete terms?**
"She doesn't want to move."

3. **Why does my mate feel this way?**
"She enjoys having around her all the things we've collected over the years, and our home holds many memories for her. If we moved to a condominium, she'd have to give up half the items we've collected, which she's not ready to do. Also, she's not ready to leave the trees, azalea bushes, and herb garden. Our yard gives her a lot of satisfaction."

4. **What will I be giving up if I don't get my way?**
"I'll be giving up considerable free time because of the house maintenance and yard work. Also, it will cost us a few thousand dollars more to stay in the house with the utilities and upkeep."

5. **Have I turned this problem into a power struggle, where having things go my way has become more important than the issue at hand?**
   "No, I haven't turned this problem into a power struggle, because although I still think it's practical to move, I'd be willing to stay. However, I'd like some of my concerns addressed."
6. **What are some alternative solutions?**
   —"Perhaps we could move if we found a condominium that would accommodate most of our things. Because we'd be giving up our yard, we might add a greenhouse."
   —"We could stay where we are, and I could hire someone to do the maintenance and the yard work, and we could adjust our spending on other items."
   —"We could look for a little smaller house where we'd have a little less space but still a yard and she could keep most of her mementos. I'd have less maintenance and yard work, and the utility bills would be smaller."

This couple opted to stay in their home, but they did hire a high-school boy to do the yard work and help with some minor repairs, and they made appropriate adjustments in their budget.

Here are some other problems that people have brought to counseling. I think you'll find their solutions quite interesting.

● It's My Money

One couple ran into a snag when the wife went back to work. She felt that the money she earned was *her* money and should be deposited in an account for her. Although most of the money she earned would be used for family expenses, she still wanted control over it. The husband thought this arrangement was unfair, since for years he had been putting his entire paycheck into a joint checking account both of them had equal access to.

The wife countered by saying that it made sense for him to put the money he earned into a joint checking account because he had been the sole breadwinner, which was his job. She had stayed home taking care of the children and the house, which was her job. Now that she was working and still handling household chores, however, she felt she was entitled to her money.

This couple discussed several alternatives. The one they both agreed on was that he would start doing a fourth of the household chores, and she would put half her salary in the joint checking account. And, if later he wanted to do half the chores, she would put her entire paycheck in the joint checking account.

● Stepdaughter Problems

Another couple had a problem over the husband's daughter from a previous marriage. He and his ex-wife had bought their daughter a car, with the agreement that he and the ex-wife split the car insurance and expenses. The plan fell through, however, and the father found himself carrying the full load. In addition, his present wife, Jane, had quit her job and gone back to school to complete her education, so money was tight.

Periodically this man would complain to his wife about money. "His complaining burns me up," said Jane, "because he won't confront his ex-wife or tell his daughter he can't afford to pay for her car and all the expenses."

I think the way this couple resolved their situation was rather unique. They made an agreement that the husband would not complain about money and that Jane would not complain about the money her husband sent to his daughter.

This solution worked well because if the husband didn't talk about money, Jane's guilt feelings about not working and not contributing financially didn't get stirred up. And if the husband was free to send his daughter money, his guilt feelings about not parenting his daughter more (she lived in another state) were not stirred up.

● An Affair *Not* to Remember

One woman came to counseling because ten years before, her husband had had an affair with a secretary in his company. He had moved out for six months and then returned home. After much trauma, anger, hurt, and discussion, this couple had decided to stay together on the condition that the husband never have another affair.

Unfortunately, the husband never apologized to his wife for the affair, but rather withdrew from her anger and hurt by burying himself with paperwork in the basement. The wife, on the other hand, never stopped talking about it. She would clip out magazine and newspaper articles on affairs and give them to her husband, along with a barrage of criticism about how could he do such a thing when she was struggling to raise the children. His affair became her obsession and it was about to drive both of them nuts.

The solution this couple worked out was that the wife agreed never again to mention, either covertly or overtly, her husband's affair. She also agreed to stop reading articles about affairs and to stop watching television programs on the subject. The husband agreed never to cheat on his wife again. He also agreed that for the next three months he would say, daily, "I apologize for hurting you, I love you, and I'm keeping my promise." The comment about "I'm keeping my promise" was his way of reassuring his wife that he wouldn't have another affair. For this couple, this solution made all the difference in their marriage.

• Lingering Bad Feelings

About four months after I started working with one couple, the wife started experiencing a lot of anger toward her husband. In therapy the husband had become more verbal, saying what he liked and didn't like. He started participating in family activities, and he became much more involved with the children—changes his wife had pleaded for in the past. The wife felt good about these changes but also resentful because it seemed that her husband had made them so easily. Since he had been so resistant to making these changes in the past, she felt he had caused her needless years of pain.

I explained that this phenomenon frequently occurs in marriage counseling. I asked the wife what her husband could do to make up for those earlier years. What would it take for her to be able to dissipate her anger? They mutually decided that he would apologize to her for thirty days. Each day he would apologize for at least one transgression in the past. Some of his apologies were for

• not being willing to go with her and the children on family outings;

• buying a motorcycle for himself without discussing it with her first;

• only putting his name on the title of the car;

• never getting up in the middle of the night and helping her with the children when they were ill.

As this husband came with his apology each day, the wife was able to let go of her anger from the past. The husband also felt better because he no longer felt guilty about his past behavior.

Another husband laid to rest his wife's periodic anger over the fact that he had never sent flowers to her in the hospital when she'd had their children. For ten days straight he brought her home a present. And she never mentioned the flowers again.

● "Let's Have Another Child"

Often in a relationship a couple will run into problems over having a child.

With one couple the wife desperately wanted another child, whereas the husband thought that one was enough and that another child would be too great a burden on them emotionally and financially. After lengthy discussions, they agreed to have another child. She promised to work a year before getting pregnant and put all the money she earned in a savings account. She also agreed to take full responsibility for the first three years of the baby's life. Both believed this was a good solution, and for this couple it worked.

Another couple ran into this same problem, but this time it was the wife who didn't want another child. They had already experienced marital problems and had been separated once, and she was afraid that two or three years after a child was born she would find herself raising the child alone. She agreed to have a child on the condition that they draw up a legal contract insuring her of so much money each month if they got a divorce. Also, their house was to be put in her name only. Clearly her issue was one of trust. Her husband agreed and they had a child.

One husband absolutely refused to have any more children. He'd had one child by a previous marriage; the wife had never had a child. The wife chose to stay in the marriage, but it took her a long time to get over her sadness. She was able to get rid of most of her bad feelings by deciding to put more energy into her own career. Also, she asked her husband to comment periodically on the sacrifice he knew she had made. This recognition from him made all the difference to her.

Most marriages can stand a situation or two where only one spouse gets his way. But if the same person gets his way too frequently, his mate will become resentful, and inevitably this resentment will cause problems in the relationship. For the spouse who always gets his way, there is also a consequence: a buildup of guilt, which he may inadvertently deal with by withdrawing from his mate.

● "I'm So Bored"

Sometimes a spouse will come to marriage counseling and say, "I'm so bored with my husband I can hardly live like this anymore. All we do is watch television night after night." So I'll ask what she would like to do. She'll reply, "Go to a movie, go dancing, take a walk, have a few friends over. Who cares? Just so we *do* something."

Then I'll ask, "Have you made these suggestions to your husband?" She'll say, "Of course, but he's always too tired or he comes up with an excuse that he has to pay the bills or do some reading for work the next day."

Finally I'll get the wife to agree that she will do things *herself* in the evening. She'll join an indoor-soccer team, and one evening a week she'll go to the movies or out to dinner with a friend.

And what happens? Two months later the husband mentions that he would like to go to her soccer game. She changed, and then he changed.

● "Why Won't You Approach Me Sexually?"

Another issue that couples disagree over is sex. Frequent issues include who approaches whom, how often do they have sex, and who's active and who's passive during lovemaking.

One woman I worked with said that she almost never approached her husband sexually, although he had frequently asked her to do so. She was quick to explain, however, that she did not consider herself a prude. Her husband laughed and said, "You are a prude." She said, "Maybe I have to be a bit of a prude because you come across like a sex maniac," to which they both laughed.

When I asked her what she meant by a "sex maniac," she said that her husband was forever telling jokes with embarrassing sexual overtones. Just recently he had told one of his famous jokes at a dinner party, and everyone just sat there with their mouths open.

I suggested that if she felt angry at her husband's behavior, she certainly shouldn't laugh when she referred to him as a sex maniac, since her laughter was inadvertently supporting his behavior. Also, I wondered if perhaps not approaching her husband in bed was her way of retaliating for the jokes he told in public. At this point he jumped in and said, "I won't tell any dirty jokes or even mention sex in public again if you'll approach me once a week." She threw her head back, laughed, and said, "You've got a deal."

This solution was perfect for this couple because they both got what they wanted and they both gave up angry behaviors that neither of them was particularly proud of.

One couple I saw for counseling hadn't had sex for over a year. Currently they were living more like roommates than husband and wife. Both had careers, both were extremely busy, and when at home their focus became the children and projects around the house. Slowly they had drifted away from each other, both emotionally and sexually. And although neither of them wanted out of the marriage, they needed to put a lot more fun in their life and start relating sexually again.

They reached the agreement that every Saturday night, despite all the projects they had going around the house, they would do something fun together. On at least two Saturday nights per month, they would do things without other couples. She would plan one week, and he would plan the next. In addition, when it was her week to make arrangements and play "social director," as they jokingly called it, she would also initiate sex.

When I would ask them in the session how things were going, it became their standard to give an embarrassed giggle and say, "Ask him, he's the 'social director' this week," or, "Ask her, she's the 'social director.'" This simple agreement made a dramatic impact on the lives of these two very shy people who had never given themselves much permission to be close, enjoy sex, and play.

Another man complained that it always seemed he wanted sex a lot more than his wife did. When we discussed this issue at length, she said that he was a good lover, he was tender, and he made sure she had an orgasm. She wasn't angry with him for other things in their life, and neither of them thought that her refusal of sex represented a power struggle or some sexual hang-up. His sexual appetite was simply greater than hers, and sometimes when he wanted sex, she was too tired. However, when she went along with her husband's desire and had sex, she admitted she enjoyed it.

I therefore suggested that she go ahead and have sex with him some of the time when he wanted it, even if she wasn't particularly interested. I still remember this woman's response: "What? Have sex when I don't want to?" I said although I don't think people should have to have sex when they don't want to, it is also important to take a look at what refusing sex time after time does to a marriage. If she enjoyed sex once she became aroused, she could decide that she would go along with her husband in this area for the good of the marriage—not always, but sometimes.

I think people often lose sight of the fact that their spouse's sexual need may be quite different from their own. If making an adjustment in this area would make for a better relationship, it would be well worth the energy.

DIVORCE: A PAINFUL ALTERNATIVE

Issues do occur in some marriages that seem to have absolutely no acceptable solution for one of the spouses. For example, what does the husband do when his wife refuses to give up the affair she's having? What does the wife do when her husband is an active alcoholic and refuses to join Alcoholics Anonymous or get treatment? What about the husband who is married to a woman who is heavily into drugs? What about the woman whose husband refuses to get a job? And what solution is there for the woman whose husband periodically beats her up? What alternatives do these people have?

Your Choice

All these people have alternatives; some are definitely more healthy. Here are some possibilities:

1. The person can choose to stay married and do nothing about the problem.
2. He can get a divorce.
3. They can go into counseling together to find out what their payoffs are for relating in this way, and then make the appropriate changes.
4. One spouse can go into counseling and change so the relationship also will change.
5. If the relationship does not change to this spouse's satisfaction, she can choose to leave the marriage with the knowledge that she has taken some responsibility for the problems in the marriage and has worked on her behavior.

A Painful but Necessary List

One of the things I do when people decide to get out of their marriage is to have them list the reasons why they made the decision to leave. This list helps them clarify what the problems have been. It also gives them support later during the ordeal of divorce, and it keeps them from discounting the problems that did exist in their marriage.

● "I Started Acting Childish"

One woman had been in counseling almost a year when she made the decision to leave her marriage. When I asked why, she wrote the following:

> It's difficult to pinpoint any one circumstance that immediately preceded the decision to leave my husband, because it was more a slow saturation, coupled with the knowledge that my children would soon all be out of the nest, leaving me to spend the rest of my life with an alcoholic who became belligerent and verbally abusive when drinking. Through counseling I have come to believe I deserve better in life. Also, my husband refused to seek treatment for his drinking. Another important factor was the realization that I was becoming bitter and childishly sought ways to "punish" him for his drinking. For example, he always refused to answer the phone when he was home, no matter what I was doing. One day I was busy cooking and the phone rang. As usual he refused to answer it, and I refused to answer it as well. We both let it ring and ring, and I remember thinking how childish I was acting just to get even with him.

● "I Became a Second-Class Citizen"

Another woman who decided to leave her husband wrote:

1. My husband doesn't like to call home to tell me he is staying out late. When I ask him where he has been, he says, "I don't have to answer to any woman."

2. I never have any free time. He always wants me to be productive. He insists that I get up at eight a.m. on weekends to clean. He highly disapproves of my sunbathing. When I go out in the backyard to

sunbathe, he comes out and starts screaming at me about how lazy I am.

3. He puts me down in public. I never feel I have any privacy, since everything I do is subject to party talk. I feel so embarrassed.

4. I have no control over my money. Until about a year ago, I gave him my entire paycheck. I was given a monthly allowance, which was to cover my medical expenses, my car payment, insurance, clothing, and lunches. He was making a lot more than I and spending it lavishly on himself.

5. He makes investments out of our joint checking account without discussing them with me, and puts them only in his name. When we bought a new car, it was only in his name.

6. His children by a previous marriage live with us half of the year. I have no say-so in how they act. Also, when the children are with us, we can't go anywhere without them. Friends invite us to dinner, and he insists we take them. And when it came time to do a will, he wanted to leave everything to his children.

7. The night after my father's funeral, he still wanted us to attend a dinner party. I didn't feel like going, so he went without me.

As this woman felt better about herself and became more independent, she made the decision to leave her husband. For no matter what approach she used, her husband seemed determined to do things "his way."

● "I Felt the Marriage Was Irreconcilable"

A man agonized in therapy for over a year before he made the decision to leave his wife. He wrote the following:

I've concluded that there were only two reasons that resulted in my decision to walk away from a marriage of thirty-three years. The first was that I met and eventually fell deeply in love with a woman who provides me with closeness and friendship and a love I never thought possible. She makes me feel wanted and good.

My second reason for ending the marriage was my unhappiness

with my wife, especially over the last ten years. We were never really friendly toward each other. Nor did we laugh much together. There was little sharing. She inherited a considerable amount of money in the beginning of our marriage, and it was always her money and in her name. If I needed money for our family, I was allowed to borrow money from her but I was to pay it back from my earnings, even if the money was for a family vacation.

We couldn't discuss problems without one of us getting angry. Our sex life was poor, and there was no day-to-day touching in our marriage. She refused to see a counselor with me.

I began having short-term affairs. I didn't purposely go looking, but if the opportunity presented itself, I took advantage of the situation. I broke the last affair off about nine years ago. When I did, the woman I was involved with called my wife and told all. My wife confronted me, and I admitted it but told her it was over. One evening after my wife had too much to drink she told the children about my affair. That night was the beginning of the end for me . . . six years ago. Within months, she moved to another bedroom, and we began separate lives in the same house. She still would not agree to seek help. The marriage became irreconcilable. Finally I did seek help, but this was after I met the other woman.

● "He Didn't Want Me Anymore"

In this situation the wife wanted the marriage to continue, but her husband didn't.

I was thirty-five, a full-time homemaker with two small children, when my husband told me he was having an affair. The shock and fear I experienced were overwhelming, so I went to counseling to find out how I could save our marriage. My husband wasn't interested in marriage counseling since he wasn't even sure he wanted to be married.

In therapy I discovered that I had been so worried about pleasing him that I wasn't pleasing myself. I had become so depressed and isolated as a young mother at home that I wasn't much fun to live with.

I got a part-time job. I worked on talking less and being less critical. My frumpy housewife image disappeared as I bought new clothes, got a haircut, and began to wear makeup. I asked my husband to start taking care of the kids and sharing in some of the housework. I began to like myself better. I became stronger and more independent, and my depression disappeared.

Ironically my husband was glad I was becoming more independent and more able to exist without him. He really didn't want to be married. I began to realize that no matter how much I tried, I couldn't make him want to be married. When he finally left, I was very sad that our family was breaking up, but I was ready to live without him.

Although it may seem that this woman had no alternatives (she wanted the marriage and he didn't), she had two alternatives. She could remain a victim and continue to feel depressed. Or she could learn to like herself more and stop holding on to a relationship that was over.

It hurts terribly when your spouse no longer wants you. But if you like yourself, even this kind of rejection is bearable.

Sometimes Necessary, but Always Tough

No matter who does the leaving, getting out of a marriage is painful. Even if the marriage is a bad one, people agonize over leaving because this says to the world that they couldn't make it work with another person. If a child is involved, there is the haunting question of what divorce will do to him. People worry about what other family members will think, what friends will be lost, and how their financial status will change. Perhaps worst of all is the fear of never being able to find anyone else and spending the rest of their life alone.

Staying in a situation where there is emotional or physical abuse or where the relationship just doesn't work for the person, however, is not a viable alternative. For when a person truly feels good about himself and has done everything possible to make the marriage better, including changing his own behavior, he will often choose divorce rather than continue to sacrifice his life to support the inappropriate behaviors of a spouse. Divorce is a tough decision with many consequences, but sometimes a person needs to use this alternative.

OTHER OPTIONS

The Want List

Although the focus of this book has been on how one spouse can make the marriage better, in a lot of marriages both people simultaneously work to make the relationship better. For these people I often suggest that each spouse draw up a Want List. The Want List is simply a list of things you want from your spouse, and a list of things your spouse wants from you.

You don't have to agree that you'll give your spouse everything he or she requests, but if you agree to fulfill the request, you write it on your list. This technique will not work if you can't discuss your issues without arguing, blaming, and redefining, but it is effective if you have cleaned up your games and have good communication skills.

Here's an example of a Want List that one couple made.

HER WANTS

1. I'd like you to make dinner Monday and Wednesday nights.

2. I'd like you to initiate social plans once a week and get a baby-sitter.

3. I'd like you to get our finances in order—check on insurance, put all our insurance policies in one place, and go to the lawyer with me to update our wills.

4. I'd like you to get the basement cleaned up.

5. I'd like you to say "I love you" once a day without me saying "I love you" first.

HIS WANTS

1. I'd like you to make dinner Tuesday and Thursday nights.

2. I'd like you to support me in my dieting.

3. I'd like you to stop calling me names when we fight.

4. I'd like you to wear some of the negligees I've bought you over the years.

5. I'd like you to come to some of my softball games.

Although these requests weren't earth shattering, they were the final touch to make things go smoothly in this marriage.

The Relationship Journal

During the course of therapy one couple changed the Want List around and came up with their own scheme for monitoring their marriage and making it work on a daily basis. They kept a legal-size pad on their kitchen table, on which they recorded the day's events. These daily recordings helped keep both of them on top of what was going on in their marriage and what they were doing or not doing to make it better.

<u>HER</u>	<u>HIM</u>
Requests of Each Other	
Decide on a restaurant for tonight.	Pick up the book I ordered.
Help me repair my bicycle.	Cut down on your requests.
Help me put weather stripping up.	
Be more firm with the doctor about your back problem.	
Acknowledgments of What My Spouse Did for Me	
Wrote a letter to our son.	Gave me a good backrub.
Was willing to hear and discuss painful issues.	Urged me to get some bed rest.
Was nice to me at dinner.	Mailed letters for me.
Listened with reflection, not suggestions.	Very helpful to me when we went to the doctor.
	Brought me my cane.
I Did This for You Because I Cared	
Accepted responsibility for communication stalemates.	Took out garbage.
Made yogurt.	Cleaned out the washbasin.
Called plumber.	Arranged to leave tickets at the box office.
Gave you a backrub.	

Little and Big Satisfactions I Had During the Day

Enjoyed wearing my new clothes.

Enjoyed looking through my new books.

Enjoyed seeing the snow on the bushes (the snow on the birdbath looked like a big cookie).

Read a book.

Went to biofeedback class.

Enjoyed a glass of beer.

I think the "Acknowledgments" part of this journal is particularly terrific because it recognizes and strokes your spouse for what he has done for you, and it helps you recognize for yourself what your spouse has done. The "Little and Big Satisfactions" entry was also important for this couple, since it helped each of them see that they had the ability within themselves to enjoy life.

I have suggested keeping this type of journal to a number of couples, and all who have done it have found it very helpful. As one man said, "If more people would work on their marriages like they work at their jobs, there would be a lot more good marriages."

ALWAYS DIFFERENCES ... AND OPTIONS

Differences in a relationship always will be present, since no two people are alike. If no disagreement ever occurs, someone is over-adapting and not taking into account their own wants and needs. When you have differences that cause a problem, keep in mind that you have several options. I think most people feel stuck and are unhappy in their marriages because they focus on the problems that they are having instead of focusing on the options available to them. Don't make this mistake ... there is always an option.

16

GRADUATION DAY

When I see someone in counseling for their last session, my feelings are truly bittersweet. Through the months we've shared some tough and wonderful times together. We've uncovered Secret Game Plans and worked on communication skills and talked about games. He has pretty much given up old ID-I-WIGD-GAR and If-It-Weren't-for-You. Now he does what he says he's going to do. He takes responsibility when a problem arises in his marriage, and he doesn't try to shift the blame and make it all his wife's fault.

We've had some great laughs together as he has shared some of his antics of earlier years. More than once I've watched him cry, and my eyes also have filled with tears as he talked of some painful things from childhood. How could his leaving not be bittersweet? He has shared so much of himself, and I've felt so close to him.

He discovered that he was Passive Aggressive, and although it's been one heck of a struggle—with me feeling irritated and him feeling defensive at my irritation—well, that's behind us now.

He asks with a grin, "Remember the time I didn't keep my list for the ninth week in a row, and you got up and dumped your entire basket of Nerf balls over my head?" I've always liked this fellow, but now I like him more because before he makes a decision, he takes into account what his wife wants and how she feels. He has learned what it means to get close.

We review how he used to compete with his wife for attention and always seemed to get the conversation back on himself and how, when his wife got sick, he found himself pouting because she was in bed. He reminds me that I told him he was acting like a spoiled brat, and how much that particular confrontation hurt him, although it jolted him into behaving more appropriately. I also know he'll never forget that confrontation, which makes me sad. But I know, too, that in looking at that behavior and changing it, he has come to have a good marriage.

He pulls out about nineteen pieces of crumpled paper in various shapes and sizes from his pocket and says, "Remember all these?" How could I forget? I certainly struggled with him to do these various assignments. He then dramatically whips out a list of things he did for his wife this past week and informs me that in four months, he hasn't missed keeping his contract of doing three nice things for her each day. Do I think he's changed? I smile and tell him I think he's changed a lot, and I ask, "Do you think you've changed?" He smiles and says, "You bet!"

He gets serious now and asks what happens if he gets stuck or there's a problem. I tell him that he will have problems on and off in his marriage. That's part of living. And sometimes he and his wife will see things quite differently. But there are solutions. And always he should start by asking the question, "What can *I* do differently to make things better?"

He nods and then asks again, but if he gets stuck can he come back? I smile and say, "Of course." If he feels stuck he should call, and we'll have a session. I'll scrape off a few barnacles and make a few confrontations, and he'll be back on track.

I remind him to make sure that he keeps spending time with his wife, talks to her, shares his hopes and dreams, and gives her compliments, and that they have sex and laugh and play together. For I know that in doing these things, he and his wife will continue to feel close and find intimacy.

I also tell him for about the hundredth time that having a good marriage means having made the decision to have a good marriage. And once that decision is made, he can use the tools and techniques that he has learned to make it happen.

He nods, and now it's time to say goodbye. He gives me a big hug and a thank-you for all the time we've spent working together, and I give him a big hug for sharing his life and thereby touching mine.

I walk out into the waiting room with him and give him one final pat on the shoulder. He bends down and gives me one final hug and says goodbye.

You, too, have sorted through a lot of things since you started reading this book. I know the information you learned didn't always make you feel so comfortable. Remember when you read the communication chapter and you said, "Oh no, I do that." And then you came to the game chapter and you became aware of the games you play. Then you reached back into your childhood and got in touch with the script messages you received. In the next chapter you saw how you play out some of these messages in your marriage. You took those tests and found out your script position and learned that sometimes you're too critical. And if that wasn't enough, you were hit with the information that you often compete with your spouse for attention, and you sometimes don't give enough positive strokes to your mate. Pretty tough stuff to admit to and then change.

But by reading this book and becoming aware of how you affect your marriage, you've already started the process of change. By continuing to follow some of the suggestions I've made along the way you will continue to change and your spouse will change in response to you. And your marriage will get better . . . and better.

Also, remember, as you change your behavior, don't forget to stroke yourself and tell yourself what a neat person you are for having the courage and putting in the energy to change. And as your spouse changes, tell her what a wonderful person she is too. In my thinking there is no finer person than one who is willing to work at getting along with another human being.

And now, it's time for us also to say goodbye. But before you close this book, I would like you to do one more thing. Take your hand, reach over your shoulder, and pat yourself on the back for all the energy you gave in reading this book and doing the exercises in order to make your marriage better. Come on, take your hand, reach over your shoulder, and pat yourself on the back. It feels good. And you deserve it!

And . . . Live Happily Ever After.

GLOSSARY

Ain't-It-Awful—A back-and-forth repartee on how difficult life can be.

Angry Righteous—The secondary script position that a person assumes in response to another's inappropriate behavior; the attitude one assumes when one feels justifiably angry. For instance, a husband promises his wife that he'll be careful of her favorite cherry tree when he paints the house. When she returns home, she finds he has cut down the tree because it was in his way. She storms into the house and refuses to go to the movie with him that night. Her position is Angry Righteous.

Attention-Competitive—A specific behavior whereby one person is competing with another over which of them is going to get taken care of, or who will get the attention in the relationship. For example, the wife gets angry with a neighbor, and the husband responds by getting twice as angry. The wife winds up trying to calm her husband down, thus taking care of him. The husband's behavior is Attention-Competitive. He is competing with his wife for attention in the relationship.

Caretaker—A person whose main focus in life is taking care of her mate. Such a person is highly attuned to the wants and feelings of her mate, while only vaguely aware of her own wants and feelings.

conditional stroke—A sign of recognition that is given for something another person has done. For instance, saying, "Thank you for picking up my shirt from the cleaners" is a conditional stroke.

Control/Attention-Competitive—A specific behavior whereby one person competes with another to be in charge of a situation and simultaneously to be taken care of. For example, the wife asks her husband a question and he says nothing. By not answering the question, the husband has control of the situation (she must wait) as well as simultaneously continuing to be the focus of his wife's attention.

Control-Competitive—A specific behavior whereby one person is competing with another over who's going to be in charge of the situation at that particular moment. For example, a man says it took twelve hours to drive to Boston, and the woman counters, "No, dear, it took twelve hours and five minutes." Her behavior is Control-Competitive. The underlying issue here is not the time it took, but who is right—who is to have the last word and be in control.

Corrector—A person who is highly critical of himself and others and whose main focus in life is to see the flaws in others and point them out.

covert message—The unspoken or underlying message that gets sent along with the spoken message. Another name for the covert message is the **hidden agenda** (see below). For example, a husband says to his wife, "Why do you read such trash?" The covert message is, "You're stupid for reading that material."

discount—An internal process whereby a person minimizes or ignores a problem, or himself, or another person.

Drama Triangle—The figure of a triangle that illustrates the three roles that people often assume in life. (See **Rescuer**; **Victim**; **Persecutor**.)

favorite feeling—The emotion that a person most often feels in response to any situation that calls forth a feeling. For example, if a person "always" feels hurt, his favorite feeling is hurt.

Game Plan—An unspoken or covert agreement between a couple that says, "when he does this, she'll do that."

hidden agenda—A message that is not stated verbally but is disguised and sent along with the more acceptable verbal message. (See **covert message**.)

negative stroke—A sign of recognition that carries the message, "You're not okay."

Nerf ball—A small foam rubber ball that comes in various colors.

nerfed—Being hit with a Nerf ball.

own/owning—Taking responsibility for one's behavior. For instance, he owned the fact he had contributed to the problem by calling his wife inappropriate names and opening her mail.

Passive Aggressive—A person whose main focus in life is himself and who continually operates from a center-of-the-world, "I count-more-than-you-count" position. Such a person takes into account his wants while discounting others around him.

Passive Taker—A person who does not focus on himself or others. As a result, such a person is only vaguely aware of his own wants and almost totally unaware of his mate's wants.

Persecutor—A person who "gets" people with angry behavior, which may take the form of a temper tantrum, a sarcastic comment, or passivity.

positive stroke—A sign of recognition that carries the message "You're okay."

primary script position—See **script position**.

Rebellious—The secondary script position that a person assumes when his or her behavior has been challenged. For example, a woman is going to her sister's wedding, and her husband pokes along until she finally decides to take her own car for fear they will arrive late. Feeling challenged, the husband decides to fix his wife and does not attend the wedding or the reception. His position is Rebellious.

redefining—Changing the topic of conversation. (See **switching the issue**.)

Rescuer—A person who takes care of another, believing he has to. Such a person discounts himself and what he wants. He also discounts the other person, who is perfectly capable of handling the situation.

script—A life plan. A group of messages a person receives, primarily in childhood, from parents, grandparents, teachers, and significant others telling the child how to live life and what to expect from it.

Script Checklist—A series of questions designed to help a person determine his or her life plan, or script.

script message—A verbal or nonverbal message that tells a child how to live his or her life and what to expect from it.

script position—One of the four positions that people assume in their relationship: Caretaker, Passive Taker, Corrector, or Passive Aggressive.

secondary script position—One of two secondary positions that people assume in their relationship in response to the behavior of another. The two secondary script positions are Angry Righteous and Rebellious.

Secret Game Plan—See **Game Plan**.

stroke—A sign of recognition: a hug, a pat, a wink, a frown, a nod, a compliment, a sarcastic comment.

subconscious—Pertaining to information or mental activity just below the threshold of consciousness. It can be brought into consciousness if one attends or attunes to it.

switching the issue—Changing the topic of conversation. (See **redefining**.)

unconditional stroke—A sign of recognition that is given for *being*. The person does not have to do anything per *se* to get this kind of a stroke. For example, "You have beautiful curly hair."

verbal Ping-Pong—A back-and-forth repartee where nothing gets decided or accomplished. This type of conversation frequently occurs when people avoid talking about the more important issues in their lives.

Victim—A person who feels helpless or is seen by others as helpless and incapable of taking care of himself.

NOTES

Chapter Two: Secret Game Plans
1. John James, M.A., "The Game Plan," *Transactional Analysis Journal*, vol. 3, no. 4 (October 1973): pp. 14–17.

Chapter Three: Communication
1. Eric Berne, *Games People Play* (New York: Grove Press, Inc., 1964), pp. 110–112.

Chapter Four: More Games
1. Eric Berne, *Games People Play* (New York: Grove Press, Inc., 1964), pp. 50–58.
2. Alvyn M. Freed, "ID-I-WIGD-GAR," *Transactional Analysis Journal*, vol. 2, no. 1 (January 1972): pp. 26–27.
3. Berne, *Games People Play*, pp. 116–122.
4. Robert Zechnich is credited with discovering this game, which he called Social Rapo. See his article "Social Rapo—Description and Cure," *Transactional Analysis Journal*, vol. 3, no. 4 (October 1973): pp. 18–21.
5. Berne, *Games People Play*, pp. 114–116.
6. Amy Harris, "Good Guys and Sweethearts," *Transactional Analysis Journal*, vol. 2, no. 1 (January 1972): pp. 13–18.
7. Berne, *Games People Play*, pp. 92–95.
8. Ibid, pp. 85–87.
9. Ibid, p. 15.
10. Ibid, pp. 112–113.

Chapter Six: Childhood
1. Eric Berne, *Transactional Analysis in Psychotherapy* (New York: Grove Press, Inc., 1961), p. 23.
2. Earl Nightingale, "It's Your Reaction," *Insight*, vol. 600-B2: p. 10.
3. The idea of asking specific questions to help people discover their script messages is credited to the work of Martin Groder, Stephen Karpman, and Claude Steiner. The Script Checklist that appears in this text was developed by the author.

Chapter Ten: Control- and Attention-Competitive
1. Jacqui Lee Schiff, *Cathexis Reader* (New York: Harper & Row Publishers, Inc., 1975), pp. 62–65. I gratefully acknowledge Jacqui Lee Schiff's material, which provided me with the basis for my theory on competitive behaviors.

Chapter Eleven: The Drama Triangle
1. Stephen B. Karpman, "Fairy Tales and Script Drama Analysis," *Transactional Analysis Bulletin*, vol. 7, no. 26 (April 1968): pp. 39–43.

Chapter Twelve: Emotions and Their Uses
1. Eric Berne, *What Do You Say After You Say Hello?* (New York: Grove Press, Inc., 1972), pp. 137–139.

Chapter Fourteen: Strokes
1. William Faulkner, *The Wild Palms* (New York: Random House, 1939), p. 324.
2. Giovanni Guareschi, *My Home, Sweet Home* (New York: Farrar, Straus and Giroux, 1966), p. 148.
3. Thomas Gordon, *Parent Effectiveness Training* (New York: Peter H. Wyden, Inc., 1970), pp. 49–61.
4. Will Durant, *The Story of Civilization: Our Oriental Heritage* (New York: Simon and Schuster, Inc., 1935), p. 429.

BIBLIOGRAPHY

American Psychiatric Association. *Diagnostic and Statistical Manual of Mental Disorders*. 3d ed. American Psychiatric Association, 1980.

Beaver, Daniel. *Beyond the Marriage Fantasy*. San Francisco: Harper & Row Publishers, Inc., 1983.

Berne, Eric. *Games People Play*. New York: Grove Press, Inc. 1964.

————. *Group Treatment*. New York: Grove Press, Inc., 1966.

————. *Transactional Analysis in Psychotherapy*. New York: Grove Press, Inc., 1961.

————. *What Do You Say After You Say Hello?* New York: Grove Press, Inc., 1972.

Bolton, Robert. *People Skills*. Englewood Cliffs, N.J.: Prentice-Hall, Inc., 1979.

Briggs, Dorothy Corkille. *Celebrate Yourself*. Garden City, N.Y.: Doubleday & Co., Inc., 1971.

Broderick, Carlfred. *Couples*. New York: Simon & Schuster, 1979.

Buscaglia, Leo. *Love*. New York: Fawcett Crest, 1972.

————. *Loving Each Other*. Thorofare, N.J.: SLACK Incorporated, 1984.

Durant, Will. *The Story of Civilization: Our Oriental Heritage*. New York: Simon and Schuster, Inc., 1935.

Faulkner, William. *The Wild Palms*. New York: Random House, 1939.

Freed, Alvyn M., "ID-I-WIGD-GAR." *Transactional Analysis Journal* 2, no. 1 (January 1972).

Garner, Alan. *Conversationally Speaking*. New York: McGraw-Hill Book Co., 1980.

Gordon, Thomas. *Parent Effectiveness Training*. New York: Peter H. Wyden, Inc., 1970.

Guareschi, Giovanni. *My Home, Sweet Home.* New York: Farrar, Straus and Giroux, 1966.

Harris, Amy. "Good Guys and Sweethearts." *Transactional Analysis Journal* 2, no. 1 (January 1972).

Harris, Thomas A. *I'm O.K.—You're O.K.* New York: Harper & Row Publishers, Inc., 1967.

James, Jennifer. *The Slug Manual: The Rise and Fall of Criticism.* Seattle: Inner Cosmos, 1984.

James, John, M. A. "The Game Plan." *Transactional Analysis Journal* 3, no. 4 (October 1973).

James, Muriel, and Dorothy Jongeward. *Born to Win: Transactional Analysis with Gestalt Experiments.* Reading, Mass.: Addison-Wesley Publishing Co., 1971.

Karpman, Stephen B. "Fairy Tales and Script Drama Analysis." *Transactional Analysis Journal* 7, no. 26 (April 1968).

Lederer, William J., and Don D. Jackson. *The Mirages of Marriage.* New York: W. W. Norton & Co., Inc., 1968.

Nightingale, Earl. "It's Your Reaction." *Insight* 600-B2.

Sager, Clifford, and Helen Singer Kaplan. *Progress in Group & Family Therapy.* New York: Brunner/Mazel, Inc., 1972.

Schiff, Jacqui Lee. *Cathexis Reader.* New York: Harper & Row Publishers, Inc., 1975.

Schiff, Aaron Wolfe, and Jacqui Lee Schiff. "Passivity." *Transactional Analysis Journal* 1, no. 1 (January 1971).

Steiner, Claude. *Scripts People Live.* New York: Grove Press, Inc., 1974.

Watzlawick, Paul. *How Real is Real?* New York: Random House, 1976.

Watzlawick, Paul, Janet Helmick Beavin, and Don D. Jackson. *Pragmatics of Human Communication.* New York: W. W. Norton & Co., Inc., 1967.

Zechnich, Robert. "Social Rapo—Description and Cure." *Transactional Analysis Journal* 3, no. 4 (October 1973).

INDEX